John Macgowan

Christ or Confucius

The Story of the Amoy Mission

John Macgowan
Christ or Confucius
The Story of the Amoy Mission
ISBN/EAN: 9783743373426

Manufactured in Europe, USA, Canada, Australia, Japa

Cover: Foto ©ninafisch / pixelio.de

Manufactured and distributed by brebook publishing software (www.brebook.com)

John Macgowan

Christ or Confucius

Missionary Manuals.

CHRIST OR CONFUCIUS, WHICH?

OR,

The Story of the Amoy Mission.

BY

REV. JOHN MACGOWAN,

MISSIONARY IN AMOY SINCE 1863;
AUTHOR OF "A MANUAL OF THE AMOY COLLOQUIAL," AND "AN ENGLISH AND
CHINESE DICTIONARY OF THE AMOY LANGUAGE."

WITH NUMEROUS ILLUSTRATIONS.

London:
LONDON MISSIONARY SOCIETY,
14, BLOMFIELD STREET, E.C.;
JOHN SNOW & CO., 2, IVY LANE, PATERNOSTER ROW, E.C.
1889.

Main Lib.
**JOHN FRYER
CHINESE LIBRARY**
BUTLER & TANNER,
THE SELWOOD PRINTING WORKS,
FROME, AND LONDON.

PREFACE.

WHEN I commenced writing the story of the Amoy Mission, I determined to confine myself simply to giving an account of the introduction of the Gospel into Amoy and the regions around, and the gradual formation and growth of the Churches there. I have consequently rigorously resisted all temptation to describe the laws and customs of the people, excepting when they were necessary to illustrate and explain my subject. In order to make the book more graphic and lifelike, I have preferred, whenever I could, to describe scenes in which I myself have mingled, and to tell the stories of men with whom I have been personally associated. This has been to me a most delightful task, as it has brought back to my recollection memories of the past, that are amongst the most pleasant in my life.

I should like to have referred to the other two Missionary Societies in Amoy—the American Mission and the English Presbyterian—and to the work that is being carried on by them, but want of space has prevented me. Even as it is, I have had to leave out all description of Hospital work, and of the growth of Self-support amongst the Amoy Churches, simply because I knew there were imperative reasons why my work should not be extended beyond the present number of pages.

If this book should, in any small degree, help to inspire the hearts of its readers with a more profound sympathy for missionary work, and should lead the Christian Churches to recognise more fully the duty and joy of sending the Gospel to their heathen brethren in China, then, indeed, would my heart's desire be satisfied, and I should be more than repaid for the time and labour I have expended upon it.

J. MACGOWAN.

LONDON, *August* 14*th*, 1889.

CONTENTS.

CHAPTER		PAGE
I.	THE GREAT PREPARATION	11
II.	AMOY AND ITS PEOPLE	25
III.	FIRST SUCCESSES	48
IV.	CHIANG-CHIU	76
V.	KOAN-KHAU	101
VI.	THE COUNTY OF HUI-AN, OR GRACIOUS PEACE	127
VII.	DITTO (*continued*)	152
VIII.	PHO-LAM	175
IX.	CONFUCIANISM, AND THE RESULTS OF MISSIONARY WORK IN AMOY	201

ILLUSTRATIONS.

	PAGE
VIEW OF THE CITY OF AMOY	*Frontispiece*
DISTRICT OF AMOY (*Map*)	10
PAGODA, GOLDEN ISLAND, HONG-KONG	15
A STREET IN CANTON	21
PEOPLE OF AMOY	29
AMOY WOMEN	35
AN OPIUM SMOKER	53
A CHINESE JUNK	83
A CHINESE LADY AT HER TOILETTE	117
SEDAN BEARERS	145
COUNTY OF HUI-AN, OR GRACIOUS PEACE (*Map*)	153
A BARBER	159
A PAGODA	177
A TEMPLE	202

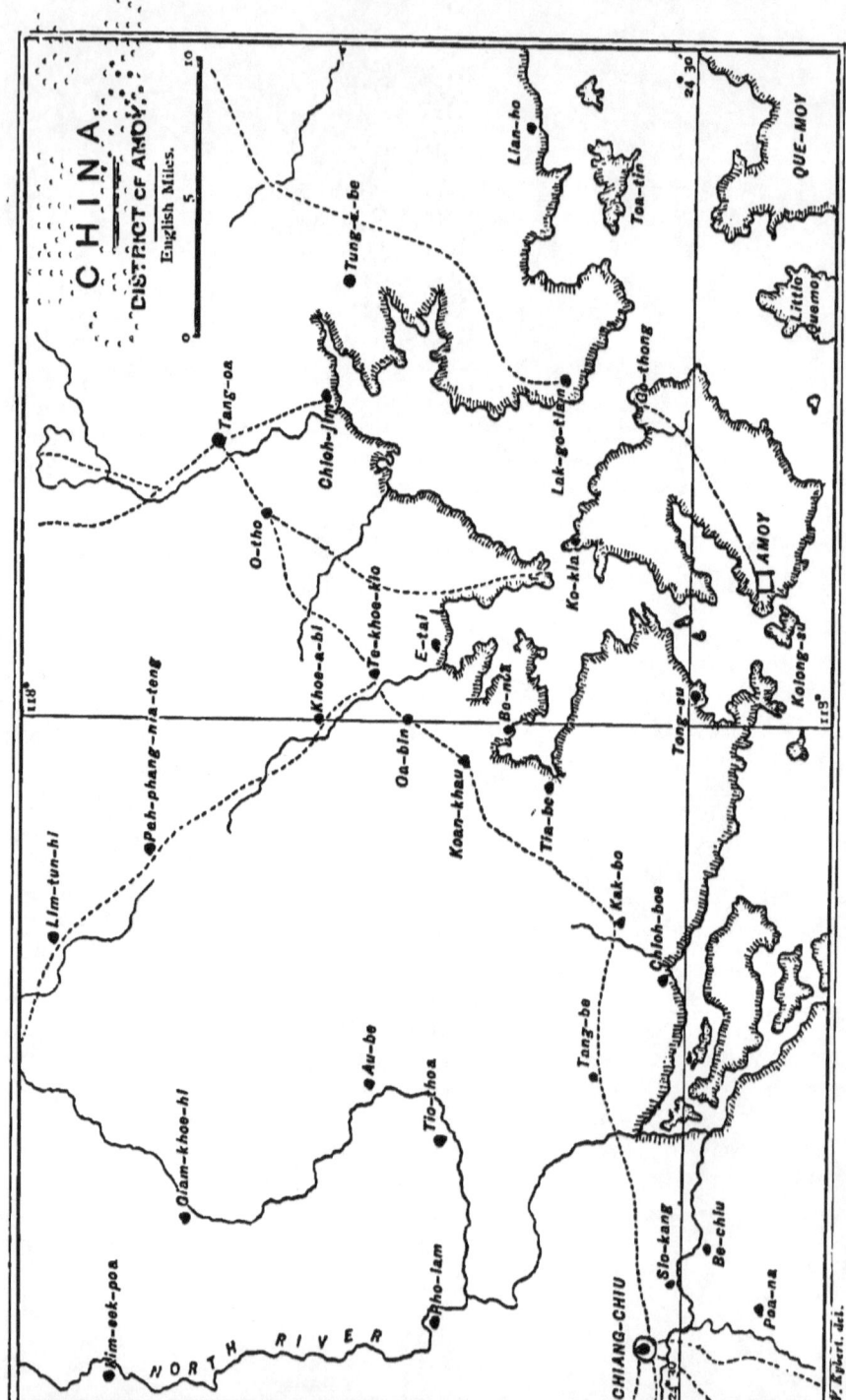

CHRIST OR CONFUCIUS, WHICH?

CHAPTER I.

THE GREAT PREPARATION.

THE dawn of the nineteenth century witnessed the first systematic efforts of any of the Protestant Churches of England to give the Gospel to the Chinese. In 1805 the directors of the London Missionary Society decided to send three or four missionaries to Penang, a possession of the English, as a preliminary step to their ultimate settlement in China. This plan was agreed upon, because a great many of the inhabitants were Chinese, and also because it was deemed hopeless to expect that any missionary would then be allowed to take up his residence in China itself. The difficulties, indeed, connected with a mission to that country were considered so insuperable, that the directors never contemplated the possibility of their men being permitted to teach and to preach. The only specific objects they dared to set before themselves were, that the missionaries should learn the Chinese language and translate the Bible into it. What should be done after these things should be accomplished it was impossible to anticipate.

On January 31st, 1807, the Rev. R. Morrison set out for China by way of America. The original intention of commencing the Mission in Penang was abandoned, through the difficulty of obtaining men. It was considered that as Mr. Morrison was going alone, he might possibly be allowed to remain in Canton until he had mastered the language. Full permission, however, was given him in his letter of instructions to remove to Penang, or to any other place that he saw fit, in case he found it impossible to remain in that city.

He arrived in Canton on September 7th, where he very soon found himself exposed to considerable annoyance and even danger. In 1808, in consequence of disputes between the English and the Chinese, he was compelled to remove more than once to Macao, which was then held by the Portuguese, so that his studies were necessarily very much interrupted. At length, seeing the risk of remaining in China to be very great, he decided to leave for Penang and study the language there. The time for his departure was actually fixed, when, on the 20th of February, he was appointed Chinese interpreter to the East India Company. This gave him an official position that secured the right of residence in China, and at the same time prevented the breaking up of the Mission in that country. The acceptance of such a post was a dangerous one, and with a different man might have meant the shipwreck of the work. With him, however, there was no risk. He had consented to become an official in order that he might the more effectually carry out the one aim which was the purpose of his life. He could now study without interruption, and, moreover, his official duties gave him such wide opportunities of getting a deeper insight into the language, that he was being continually qualified for the great work of translating the Scriptures into Chinese.

Although public preaching was not allowed, he availed himself of every opportunity for making known the Gospel to those who came within his immediate influence. The Chinese in those early days were not easily moved to become Christians. The utter contempt with which they were accustomed to look down upon the foreigner made them scout the idea that he had anything better to teach them than what they had received from their great sages. China was the land of light and culture and refinement, and had nothing to learn from the outer barbarian. The idea of one of these coming to teach the Chinese was just as ludicrous as though a Zulu were to come to London, and, establishing himself in some prominent position, were to invite the scholar and the scientist to sit at his feet and be instructed by him. Now the conceit and haughty insolence which were marked features in the Chinese character were to be found in a more intensified form amongst the Cantonese, than perhaps in any other part of China. It was therefore particularly unfortunate that the first contact of the missionary with the Chinese empire should have been at Canton. This city was one of the most prominent in the country. There were others that could excel it in the beauty of their natural surroundings, and in the historic memories that clustered around them, but it stood pre-eminent as one of the strong cities of the empire. The lofty walls that surrounded it, and the massive gates, through which the teeming crowds passed in and out, had an imposing air of strength that seemed to bid defiance to all the world, and to laugh to scorn any attempt that might be made to capture them. It was one of the wealthiest places in the kingdom. Like other Chinese cities, it had its narrow lanes, where the poorer people lived, and long lines of streets where the smaller shops were opened; but it was conspicuous for the number of its large and extensive business houses, where trade on a large scale was carried on. Here could be found, as hardly anywhere else in the empire, firms where the finest silks and satins, and elegant embroidery of every design, could be procured. Not only articles of native manufacture could be bought, but also those from far-off distant cities, which had been carried over lofty mountains and down great rivers to this famous mart. Here, too, were to be found the most beautiful vases from well-known potteries, painted with the most exquisite colours, the secret of which was known only to their designers, and which has since been lost to the world. Tea warehouses, filled with the fragrant leaf that came from the centre of China, to be shipped away to England, explained in some measure the presence of the English ships that lay anchored in the river. The city was alive and bustling, and had the air of a pressure of business upon it. Men from the region around, and from the far interior provinces, could be seen in its streets. Tea merchants from Hankow, silk merchants from Soochow, makers of the famous pottery from the Kiangsi province, merchants from distant cities coming to buy and sell, mandarins of all degrees with their retinues, and speaking the different dialects of their far-off homes, so that they were strangers in language amongst the very people they had come to rule, all spoke of the hold that this mighty city had upon remote places in the empire.

PAGODA, GOLDEN ISLAND, HONG-KONG.

The people of Canton were perhaps the most vigorous in the kingdom. Though bred and born within the tropics, and scorched by the great Eastern sun for the greater part of the year, the only effect seems to have been to develop in them an extraordinary amount of mental and physical ability. In their build, they could not compete with those of some of the northern provinces, but in push and enterprise and business capacity they stood first amongst the men of the eighteen provinces. They were men of daring, too. Their trading junks were accustomed to make considerable voyages along seas where gales are frequent in winter and typhoons in summer. The China Sea, and the Formosa Channel, swarmed with pirate junks manned by Cantonese, and none so terrible and ruthless as they. No force could compete with them, and it has required the naval power of England to rid the seas of these monsters.

The consequence of all this was, that the people of Canton were a proud and haughty race. They felt themselves more than a match for any of their own countrymen, and much more therefore for the barbarian English. Even at the present day, after successive defeats, and the capture and occupation of their city by English troops, the Cantonese still behave with a rudeness and arrogance such as are experienced in no other place where Europeans have been accustomed to reside for any length of time. One can easily understand, therefore, how dreary and depressing the early years of the first missionary's life must have been. Active work, such as is openly carried on to-day, would not have been tolerated, either by the Chinese authorities or by the directors of the East India Company. In patient waiting and strong faith in God, and in the Divine power of the Gospel, he had come to preach; in these alone could he find a comfort for his soul; and by the grace of God he never faltered in his purpose or dreamt of giving up the enterprise as hopeless.

The year 1813 proved to be a memorable one in

the history of the Mission. After six years of solitary labour by Morrison, the Rev. W. Milne arrived in China to become his colleague, and for the few years he was permitted to live did splendid service, the fruits of which remain to the present day. But the great event of the year was the completion of the translation of the New Testament into Chinese. Men who were ignorant of that language had argued that it was impossible to put the wondrous thoughts, and subtle shades of meaning, and the tender and pathetic language of the Bible into those cumbrous Chinese characters. As though God had given a revelation that could never be communicated to fully a fourth of the human race! Men forgot that the Bible is an Oriental book, full of figures and similes, and teeming with illustrations from Nature that can be understood best under an Eastern sky. In coming to China it was nearer its home than it was where dreary winters and leaden skies prevail. The Chinese language is one of the most beautiful in the world in which to enshrine the sacred Scriptures, and there is a flexibility and grace about it, that render it capable of expressing all the tenderness, and pathos, and poetry, and sublime thought of that most wondrous book.

Morrison himself was deeply impressed with the work he had done. What a comfort and a joy he must have felt as the last sheets were printed, and the Word of God, the revelation of Jesus Christ, was now ready to be distributed amongst the Chinese. He had not been allowed to preach. He had been watched and suspected. Edicts forbidding the Chinese to receive the religion of the foreigners had been issued. "A special express was sent from

Peking for search to be made for persons professing the Christian religion, and old people and country gentlemen were called upon by the Government to give information against such." Anything that was done by him had to be effected as quietly as possible, for any public manifestation would have been attended with danger to himself, and to those who listened to him. Little did those in power dream that he had already completed a work that one day would revolutionize China, and change her customs, and break up the long sleep of ages, and give men thoughts such as no sage had ever taught them. The Word of God was now ready to do a work that no mandarin or royal edict could stop. God's message, selfishly held back by the Christian Church for so many ages, had at last reached China, and men's hearts, there recognising the Divine voice, would ere long respond in loving and loyal service to Him.

The next great event in Morrison's life was the baptism of the first Chinese convert on July 16th, 1814. "At a spring of water," he says, "issuing from the foot of a lofty hill by the seaside, away from human observation, I baptized Tsae-a-ko in the name of the Father, Son, and Holy Spirit." What a day of rejoicing this must have been! For nearly seven years he had hoped, and longed, and prayed for this very thing. Men had said: You cannot convert the Chinese; and when he saw the arrogance and scorn with which the Chinese scouted the idea of being instructed by a barbarian, he must have had his moments of perplexity and depression. But after years of weary waiting, the Gospel has proved its old power. And now he receives the firstfruit of that mighty harvest that other labourers will reap in the future.

It would be interesting to learn what was the attractive power in Christianity that led this Chinaman to give up his idolatry, and his ancestral worship, and to run the risk of death at the hands of his rulers. Fortunately we have his own written confession, and we are not surprised to find that the one feature of the Gospel that touched his heart was the same that had so mightily taken possession of the mind of Paul, and had become the ruling force in his life, and that was, Christ and Him crucified. He says that "Jesus has made an atonement for us is a message that is full of joy. Language and thought are both inadequate to exhaust the gracious and admirable goodness of this purpose of Jesus. I now believe in Jesus, and rely on His merits to obtain the remission of sin. I have sins and defects, and without faith in Jesus for the forgiveness of sins I should be eternally miserable." How wonderfully this man speaks of sin, who never knew what the word meant till he heard the Gospel! Christianity had given him a definite conception and sense of the evil that was in his life, and had shown him the way to get rid of it. Confucius had never done this, and no voice from the great temples in the city had ever suggested it. The cross with its Divine story had revealed to him his misery and his salvation, and so his confession centres round Christ who had delivered him.

The men and women that have been converted since have all followed in his footsteps. As I listen to his confession it has a strangely familiar sound to me. I know its language; I can hear the very tones and accents in which it was uttered, for I have baptized hundreds of Christians, and they have all seemed instinctively to adopt this same grand confession of faith.

And so the years went by amid struggles and difficulties. Everything had to be done with the utmost secrecy and caution, lest the Chinese Government should take action against him. He knew that his own countrymen would not stand by him and uphold him in such a case, for the East India Company, having heard that he had translated the New Testament and various tracts into Chinese, sent out an order that his connection with them should be severed, for "they were apprehensive that serious mischief might possibly arise to the British trade in China from these translations."

In the meantime as there was no scope for missionary work in China, missions were commenced in Batavia, Malacca, Penang, and Singapore, amongst the Chinese residing there. One very valuable result of this was that men were being trained in a knowledge of Chinese and of Chinese life that would specially qualify them to be workers in China the very moment that country was opened. And splendid men were some of these, and well adapted for the great work that was to be done by and by; one of the mightiest empires in the world was to be won for Christ. Men of feeble hands, or still feebler hearts, would fail in the enterprise, and so God selected, in this crisis, men of great powers of mind, and of still profounder faith. Such names as Morri-

A STREET IN CANTON.

son, Milne, Medhurst, Legge, Stronach and Lockhart, will be imperishably connected with the first preaching of the Gospel in China.

In 1834 Morrison died; Milne had finished his work twelve years before. Soon after his death the mandarins began to enforce more rigidly their regulations against the intercourse of Chinese with foreigners, and also against their belief in Christianity. The little band of Christians were punished by fines and imprisonment, and were released only by the payment of a large sum of money, which Mr. J. Morrison, who had succeeded his father as Chinese Secretary, very generously paid. The Chinese pastor Leang-a-fa, found it expedient under these circumstances to leave China and fly to Malacca. It began to look as though this missionary enterprise were to be a failure. The founder of the work was dead. For twenty-seven years he had given his soul to it, but he was gone now, and those who had been gathered by him, were left to the tender mercies of the heathen. The strong and merciless hand of the law had been laid upon the Christians, and they were scattered as sheep without a shepherd. China, with its ancient civilization and its great sages and teachers, and with its stronger than adamantine walls that were reared so high, as if to keep out the very sounds that might come in from the outside world, will never be evangelized. These strong men, with the mighty forces behind their backs, will never give up the traditions and teachings of their fathers. Christianity will have to retire before such invincible forces. Will it? The time is very near when these walls shall be rent, and Christianity shall stand face to face with the nation. The appliances are all ready. The Bible has been translated, and men of indomitable faith are waiting, all ready trained for the conflict. No gathering of great armaments has been seen, no clash and sound of weapons being forged in the workshops of the world have been heard, and no assembling of troops witnessed, and yet there have been forces prepared that shall not fail in their conquest of China.

In August 29th, 1842, by treaty with the Chinese emperor, Hong-Kong was ceded to the English, and Canton, Amoy, Foochow, Ningpo, and Shanghai became open ports, where men of every nation might freely reside. Our missionaries, who had been eagerly looking for this, at once hastened to enter China, and Hong-Kong and Shanghai were occupied as mission centres, whilst two years afterwards the wondrous work, whose story will be told in the following pages, was commenced at Amoy.

The weary years of waiting are ended. The dawn has come at last. The shadows are beginning to tremble before the coming day, and soon along the coast, and far away into the interior, across its plains and among its mountains and valleys, shall the light flash, till the darkness shall have vanished, and Christ come to claim the kingdom for His own.

CHAPTER II.

AMOY AND ITS PEOPLE.

THE island of Amoy is on the southern coast of China, about three hundred miles to the north-east of Hong-Kong. It is about thirty miles in circumference, and is beautifully situated in the midst of a very extensive bay. Seaward, it is protected by a chain of islands, the largest and most important of which is about the size of Amoy, and is called Quemoy, or "The Golden Gate." This acts as a natural breakwater, and prevents the heavy seas that are raised by storms and typhoons from rolling into the bay and injuring the shipping that lies anchored there.

On the south the bay is bounded by a low range of mountains, from the midst of which rises abruptly Lam-tai-bu, the "Great Southern Warrior." This is the most beautiful sight in the whole of the landscape, for there is a never-ending charm in its varying moods, as seen in storm or sunshine. In fine weather its summit is bathed in great floods of light, and it stands out clearly against the sky as it looks down upon the blue waters of the bay, which dance and sparkle beneath the rays of the great eastern sun. When bad weather is coming on, dense masses of cloud, tumultuous and agitated, as if clinging to it for protection, gather round its head and far down its sides, and then the waters of the bay, dark with the shadows cast upon them, seem to be in sympathy with them, as though they feared the coming gale.

To the west and north the scenery is very grand and rugged. It seems to consist entirely of hills and mountains, for the plains and valleys that lie at their feet, and that contain cities and villages and great market towns, are hidden from our view till we come upon them. The hills have grouped themselves into all kinds of imaginable shapes. Over the lower grounds can be seen the peaks that tower above the rest; whilst one range of mountains rises above another, till the distant background seems to be resting against the sky.

The city of Amoy is a walled town of the third degree in rank. As compared with the great cities of the empire, such as Canton, Suchow, or Hang-chow, it is a very small and insignificant place. It is a dull, semi-respectable town, and all the business and life and energy that the Chinese are capable of are concentrated in the immense suburbs that have absorbed nearly all the wealth and trade of the port. These are very finely and picturesquely situated. They stretch along the shore of the beautiful bay, which is lighted up daily with almost perpetual sunlight.

The harbour is diversified by junks and sailing vessels, and all kinds of steamers on their way north or south; whilst one ship that flies the white flag of England shows that one of our men-of-war has come from our far-off home to guard and protect us if needs be.

The scene before us is a busy one. The steamers, with great noise and clatter, and with a rapidity that the Chinese coolies do not relish, are discharging their cargoes. They are in a hurry to be off, and, moreover, all this incessant rush and activity are but in keeping with the restless and untiring energy of the Englishman. Close beside them is a huge junk hoisting its great mat sail, to the slow, monotonous song of the sailors. This song, which might have been composed in the days of Confucius, has not yet caught the spirit of the nineteenth century. There is no inspiration about it, nor anything to warm the men's hearts and cause them to pull the sail up to the masthead with a rush. A little farther on a number of sailors are standing on the bow of another junk beating gongs. They begin with measured strokes, and end with a few given quickly and with great energy. They are welcoming a junk that is coming in with flowing sail from sea, and they are expressing the gladness of themselves and their shipmates that they have passed safely through all the perils of the deep. Passage boats of all sizes and descriptions are coming in from the country districts laden with passengers, small boats plying for hire from the shore to the shipping dot the bay, and see! here is a boat's crew from the man-of-war, and Jack, with his easy, saucy air, seems as much at home as though he were crossing the Solent.

The town is a thoroughly typical one, and from it we can, in a large measure, judge what is the character of nearly every other one in the country. To enable the reader to get an idea of what it is like, I shall take him through one of the principal streets, and let him see some of the scenes that may be constantly witnessed in it. This street, being an important one, is wider than the generality, but even it is not more than about fourteen feet; but as most of the shops have projecting counters, on which goods are displayed, the really available space for the public is often not more than from eight to ten feet. The crowd in this street is always dense; and were it not that it is usually good-natured, and careful in following the rule of the road, there would be fierce collisions and stoppage of the traffic. Such narrow streets, where so much of human life has to pass in such close contact the livelong day, would never suit the people of the west, where men are high-spirited and easily take offence, and where the exigencies of life make it difficult for them to brook delay.

But it is not the people only that pass along these narrow arteries. Everything that the necessities of the town require has to be conveyed along them. As we are sauntering quietly along with the crowd, a faint shout is heard in the distance, which grows louder and still more loud as it approaches us. We discover that it proceeds from four men who are carrying an immense bale of Manchester cottons on bamboo poles, the ends of which rest on their shoulders. Their cries are to warn the people to get out of the way, and speedily this must be done, for they come along at a swinging trot, and a blow from the ends of the poles, or from the heavy bale might prove a serious matter to the person struck. The crowd good-naturedly opens up a way to let them pass, whilst we hurriedly flatten ourselves against a fruit-stall. The men swing by us with a shout, and are almost instantly lost in the human tide in which they are engulphed, but their voices can still be heard in the distance, long after they have disappeared from sight.

PEOPLE OF AMOY.

We now come to a part of the road that is slightly wider than the rest. At the side of it is a man seated at a small table, on which are laid materials for writing. Two ink-slabs, one for black and the other for red ink, are placed in order before him. He is a man of about fifty years of age, with large spectacles on his nose, and he assumes a learned look, as though he would try and persuade the public that he belongs to the literary class. He is wanting, however, in that invisible something that marks the true scholar, and consequently no one is deceived by him. He is a broken-down tradesman perhaps, or a ne'er-do-weel who had been partially educated when he was young, but who had not character enough to go on with his studies. He is now picking up a very precarious living by writing letters for the very poor and uneducated classes of society. But let us draw near, for a woman has just come up to his table, evidently on business, and custom will allow us to stand by and listen to what she has to say. The letter-writer has now assumed a learned look, and he peers over the spectacles at her with an air of profound thought, as she tells him what she wishes him to write about. She wants him to write a letter to her son, who has gone abroad, and has not written to her for a very long time. She then tells a long story of how good her son was as a boy, how filial he was, and with what affection he used to treat her. The mother's heart is full, and her eyes glisten as she speaks of those happy days, and the virtues of her son. Then her voice changes, and a cloud comes over her face as she proceeds to tell how evil companions got hold of him and worked his ruin. He gave up his work, became a gambler, and then an opium smoker, and finally left the country in the hope of turning over a new leaf, and of finding a fortune that could not be got in Amoy. She tells her story with great dramatic effect. At one time her eyes are filled with tears, as the painful memories are recalled, then her features assume a stern and angry appearance, as she recounts the wiles by which her son was led astray. Then her face brightens as she speaks of her hopes that her son may yet repent, and come back to her home to be a comfort to her. The people who have gathered round the table, attracted by our presence, listen sympathetically. They nod their heads and look pleased when she speaks of her once happy home, and they utter very strong, unclassical language when she describes some particular individual whose influence had been the ruin of her son. The letter-writer listens quietly, but with a dignified manner, as the tragic story is being rehearsed. He is human, however, for, as we watch him, we see that his feelings get the better of his reserve, and looks of pity, and anon of indignation, steal over his face, as the woman acts out this most piteous story of her life. After she has concluded he proceeds to write the letter. The paper is soon covered with strange hieroglyphics in perpendicular columns, written with black ink. Then the stops are all put in with red ink, and important sentences underlined with the same, and finally it is read over to her to see whether it contains all she desired to say. It is then folded up and addressed, and for all this he receives the modest sum of one penny.

Again we saunter on. We pass by opium shops, always dingy and dark looking, as though they feared the light of day, and silk shops, and idol carvers, and fruiterers, and eating houses, where groups of hungry customers are shovelling basinfuls of suspicious-looking stuff down their throats with chop sticks. A large cauldron is kept ostentatiously boiling in front of these houses, and the steam that rises from it is a capital advertisement to the hungry passers-by. For a penny one can dine luxuriously whilst standing round the cauldron.

These main streets are capital places for seeing how the Chinese live. Everything is open to the public. What they talk about, what they eat, how they spend their time, and how hard the majority of them have to work can all be seen by a quiet walk down any of them. It is amazing in what a narrow space a Chinese family can live, and how many families can be accommodated in a house that, according to our ideas, is capable of giving room to only one. Let us stop and look at the one just close by us. It is about twenty feet deep and ten feet wide. The man that occupies it is a locksmith. In front is his stock-in-trade, and immediately within is a bench on which he is sitting with two young lads, his apprentices, busily engaged in making iron hinges. Immediately beyond them is the wife with a baby in her arms, and two little ones playing on the floor. This is their home, where their lives are spent. During the summer the place is stiflingly hot, and it is a mystery to us how human beings can live and seem moderately happy in such a terrible atmosphere. I presume they have not much time to think about the heat. The great problem with them is how they shall earn enough to pay the rent, and feed and clothe the family.

The pleasures they enjoy are very few. As they

know nothing of the Sunday, every day is a work-day to them. There are certain national festivals, however, when the noise of labour ceases, and the family, dressed out in their best clothes, make it a business to enjoy themselves. The tools are laid aside, and the weary workman sits calmly smoking his pipe, looking out on the moving world before him, absorbed in the business of taking rest. But he cannot change his surroundings, for these are always the same. The dirty, narrow street outside, with the everlasting tread of men passing by, never changes. The house too, with its dirty walls and earthen floors, impossible to be kept clean, reminds the family continually of their poverty. The green fields are miles away. They would like to look upon them, but they are too far distant. The great sun shines overhead, and at certain times of the day his rays flash in on the dingy walls, and play about the dirty floor, and light up the cage in which the lark is hung, and touch with a passing glory the solitary flower they are rearing; but they seldom see him as he is setting in the west, filling the clouds with exquisite colours, and flashing his golden rays over mountain peaks and ranges, as a farewell message to the world before he leaves it in darkness.

Whilst we are standing looking at this shop, we are conscious of strange sounds that reach our ears above the hum of the people in the shops around us, and of the tread of the passing crowds. We hear the violent beating of gongs, and then a long-drawn sound of "I-yo," uttered by a number of voices. We notice, too, that the crowd, going in the direction of the sounds, begins to scatter, and the people range themselves at the sides of the road, faces outwards, and their arms hanging respectfully by their sides. A mandarin with his retinue is approaching, and we must stand where we are, for we must show him the respect that is due to his rank. The men that uttered the prolonged sound are the lictors that precede the great man, and with whips in their hands they clear their way in a rough and ready fashion, should any one be incautious enough to get into it. The appearance of these men is highly provocative of mirth. Their hats are exactly like fools' caps, and sit sideways on their heads. This gives them an exceedingly comical appearance, though the Chinese do not think so. The question here arises: Why should a tall fool's cap set awry on a person's head provoke a smile in us, when three hundred millions of people look on the same sight and see nothing funny in it? They are a villainous-looking set of men, and every one of them seems as if he had come out of the opium den, for the opium hue is on their faces. Their whips are poised ready for instant use, the prospect of which they seem to enjoy. They cast their eyes furtively from side to side, upon the standing lines of people, and there is a sour dissatisfaction in their faces, because they cannot get a chance at them. But look! here is a country bumpkin, fresh from his fields, and slow in his movements, who has dared to cross the road in front of them. The dark, forbidding faces light up with a gleam of satisfaction, and whack! whack! whack! and he is taught a lesson in etiquette that he will not soon forget.

After these men come a crowd of ragged urchins, veritable street arabs, who for a penny or so have

AMOY WOMEN.

been hired for the occasion to carry large boards, on which are inscribed the office and titles of the mandarin. They are impudent little fellows, bubbling over with fun and mischief, and they grin and make hideous faces at us, as they pass close by. Behind them come men carrying chains, dread emblems of the power of the magistrate, and intended to strike terror into the hearts of evildoers. Closely following upon them comes the great man, seated in his sedan chair, which is carried by four bearers. He is a thoroughly typical-looking man of his class, for he is very stout, and he has a very dignified, magisterial air about him, which he never loses for an instant. If the scenes before him touch him at all, he is careful to conceal the slightest traces of emotion. There is not a ripple on his face, and not the slightest sign that he has the remotest sympathy with those he rules. Their very language is a mystery to him, which he cannot understand, for it is one of the laws of the present dynasty that no man may be a mandarin in his own district. This man comes from a distant province, where a different language is spoken, and the probability is that his thoughts even now are in his far-off home, amongst his kindred there, and that he sees nothing of the strange sights around him.

The crowd that has been pent up, during the passage of this official procession, now surges into the middle of the road, and, with quickened pace, tries to make up for lost time. As we are not in a hurry, we walk along leisurely. We have not progressed very far before our ears are assailed by a terrible din of cymbals and small drums. Very soon we come to a large crowd that packs the street so densely that further progress is absolutely stopped. A theatre has been planted in this, one of the busiest streets of the town. For forty or fifty yards on each side of it the people are packed like herrings, gazing with rapturous, upturned faces at the actors. They are just concluding a farce, and ever and anon bursts of laughter show how keenly the fun is appreciated by the crowd. When this is concluded, a famous historical play is performed, and ere long mandarins and soldiers in the dress of an ancient dynasty are in mortal conflict, and the crowd is hushed, and holds its breath, and the gaze is long and intense, as they await the result of the battle. To give intensity to the scene, the cymbals break in at certain times with furious clashing, and the drums rattle as though in the midst of a hot engagement. To an unpractised ear this is exceedingly annoying, for the voices of the actors are completely drowned, and to us there is nothing but dumb show. The Chinese, whose musical ear has been trained by ages of such music, are entranced with the hideous noise. We are disgusted; but what does the ear of a barbarian know of music? It is as untrained as his mind, and needs the civilizing influence of the "Middle Kingdom" to teach it to appreciate really good sounds, such as crash out from these vile cymbals.

The acting before us is first-rate, for the Chinese are natural, born actors, but it is exceedingly grotesque. Even a serious play is full of suggestions of mirth to a foreigner, and he will often be convulsed with laughter, whilst the crowd is hushed into seriousness. What specially strikes one about these actors is the coolness and ease with which they perform their parts, and the natural life-like way in which they act the characters they have taken. Two women for example are quarrelling and scolding each other. As women are not allowed to be actors, two men have assumed their dress. The looks, the gestures, the feminine toss of the head, the rising tones that grow shriller and shriller as their passions become excited, are exactly such as may be witnessed in the quarrels of women almost any day in the streets of Amoy. We forget, in the reality of the scene before us, that these persons are actors. They have impersonated an actual event in human life so realistically, that the stage seems to have vanished, and we are standing in one of the narrow streets of the city, with the crowd around us, watching two women so completely absorbed by their passions as to have become oblivious of the many eyes that are fastened upon them.

It is certainly amusing, the complete way in which this theatre has taken possession of the street. Coolies come up with huge loads on their shoulders, whose destination lies perhaps a few yards on the other side of it, but no way is made for them. Sedan chairs, with their fares, are carried within a few feet of the crowd, but the bearers, with a half-sullen half-good-natured look upon their faces, turn back to find their way by another street. The whole traffic is stopped, but there is no grumbling, no row, and no outcry of any kind. This custom of acting on the streets is the growth of long ages, and the Chinese are too wise to grumble at something that they dearly love, and which, moreover, they can always see for nothing.

Thus far I have been endeavouring to give some

idea of Amoy and its surroundings. To complete the picture, I must now speak somewhat more definitely of the people, amongst whom missionary work was about to be commenced.

The men of Amoy and of the region around are a bold, independent race, very vigorous both mentally and physically. They have a reputation which extends far beyond their own country, for their poverty has compelled large numbers to emigrate to other countries, to endeavour to find a subsistence that they cannot get in their own land. They are *brusque* and rough in their manners, very often to rudeness. They speak out their minds with great freedom, and, to one who is not accustomed to their manners, offensively. They are without that polish and suavity that their countrymen in other parts of China have to perfection. Even after many years' residence amongst them it is difficult sometimes not to believe that their rough ways of addressing or answering are intentionally insulting. You want something done in a particular way, for example. They will not hesitate at once to express their opinion about its stupidity, if it should strike them as wanting in wisdom. Some statement is made which seems to them to be very doubtful, though you are absolutely certain that it is true. They will at once declare there is not a shadow of truth in what you say. They are accustomed in ordinary life to speak to each other in this way, and though their innate sense of propriety will restrain them up to a certain point, their independence of character will eventually assert itself, and they will express themselves in a way that is oftentimes exceedingly offensive. This of course refers to the common people. The educated classes are more refined, and therefore more careful as to their manner of expressing themselves.

There is one very offensive feature about the Chinese, that is not simply annoying in itself, but that has always been a serious hindrance to the immediate reception of the Gospel in any place where it is first preached, and that is the deep-rooted scorn and contempt they have for the foreigner. It is difficult for any one who has merely read of this to understand all that is meant by this statement. To get a thorough idea of what this feeling is, one has to pass through a great city, where the foreigner has seldom been seen. The streets are thronged with an ever continuous stream of people; but though you move and mingle amongst the crowd, you feel there is not an atom of sympathy that binds you to any one in it. You rub shoulders with the people, but mighty oceans might roll between you, and great ranges of mountains divide you, so sharply separated are you from any kindly feeling on their part. They gaze upon you as they would upon any strange animal that had suddenly appeared amongst them. The most contemptuous expressions flash from mouth to mouth. The shopkeepers crowd to see you pass. Their faces exhibit not merely curiosity, but open and undisguised contempt, and low guffaws reach your ears from the shops on each side of the street. To be thus absolutely cut off from all kindly sympathy with one's fellow-creatures, and to be a solitary unit amidst vast crowds, gives one an oppressive feeling of loneliness, such as no desert could produce. You catch at last what you fancy is a friendly face amidst the host of sneering contemptuous ones, and your heart warms at the sight. Or perhaps you are jostling your way along, weary and heart-sore, when a man suddenly accosts you. He is full of kindly greetings, and he shows by the hearty, demonstrative way in which he addresses you that he is rejoiced to see you. You feel as if you could embrace the man upon the spot for very gladness of heart. You recognise him as a former patient at the hospital with which you are connected. You were able to do him some kindness during his sickness, and he remembers it. As you stand chatting with him, the crowd stops too. They want to know what you are talking about. The man rehearses, for their benefit, all the favours he has received from you. He tells them he was sick, nigh unto death, and how the foreign physician saved his life. He speaks of the attentions you were able to pay him, and the little comforts you gave him, and as the picture rises before him of those weary days in the hospital when the shadow of death lay upon him for some time, he becomes quite eloquent in your praises. The crowd becomes sympathetic. The sneer dies out of their faces. There is nothing that touches the Chinese heart so mightily as practical benevolence. It is a virtue they highly appreciate. Their stolid, emotionless features begin to light up with genuine feeling, and the eyes of some are twinkling and flashing as their hearts are moved by his story. You feel the inspiration of the change, and your heart goes out in loving hope to those who but a minute or two ago seemed separated from you by an impassable gulf. You bid the man good-bye, and the crowd silently melts into the human stream, and again you hurry on your way. Soon the epithets are as vile, and the jeers of the people as loud as ever, but they do not sting as they did a while ago. The incident that has just happened has been a mighty revelation. It has brought you closer to the Chinese heart than you were before, and it has revealed to you the wondrous possibilities of the future when that shall have been touched by the love of Christ.

This contempt for the foreigner, though deep enough amongst the masses, is still more profound amongst the scholars of the country. They are consequently the most formidable enemies the missionary has to deal with. It might have been supposed that education would have made them more liberal in their views than the uncultivated farmers and artisans, yet this is not the case, but actually the reverse. Their education, instead of enlarging their minds, has the positive effect of cramping them. A thoroughly educated man may have no independent views that will clash with the teaching of past ages. He is not allowed to propound any thoughts that are not sanctioned by their sacred classics. His face is always turned to the past, for there, he believes, lies the source of inspiration to himself and his nation. The future has no word of hope or comfort for him, for it is shrouded in an impenetrable mystery. The past he knows something of. The great sages, with their writings that have made China what it is, live there. Their forms, it is true, are misty and shadowy, and more than twenty centuries hide them from his gaze, but they are the only force he knows in life that has given him thought. When he turns to the future he looks into a vacancy, where no figure is seen, and no voice breaks the silence to tell the story.

But let us imagine for a moment one of these scholars standing before us. He is dressed in a long robe that comes down to his ankles. This is usually made of coloured silk, or common homespun calico, dyed with the universal blue, just according to the means of the man. His head is cleanly shaved, and his *queue* plaited with extreme care, whilst in his right hand he holds a fan, with which, with natural ease and dignity, he gracefully fans himself. His face is a perfect picture, because it is in striking contrast to those that one sees at a glance belong to the great unwashed around. It is keenly shrewd and intelligent. The black eyes snap and sparkle at the bidding of hidden thoughts that come only to men of his class. How his brain teems with traditions, that reach away back until they touch the region where history is lost, and myths and romances reign supreme. Sages, and poets, and statesmen, and great warriors, and mighty emperors troop by, solemn and ghostly, but their words and deeds still live, and he believes there is no country with so grand a history as that of China. He is very proud and scornful, and the way he can curl his lip, and compress into that pale face his contempt for the barbarian, is very trying to one's temper. We speak to him of moral questions, and he seems at once to be in his element. He will quote the finest passages in the writings of the sages that touch upon these. The beauty of virtue is dwelt upon, lovingly and sympathetically as it seems, and pearls drop one by one from his mouth, and we instinctively say: What a splendid fellow this is! He is nothing of the kind.

His education has trained him to talk this way, but his heart is unmoved by the words of the great men he has been quoting, and when it comes to a question of money-making he will act as though he were utterly destitute of principle. He uses his education simply as a lever to gain his own ends. He foments quarrels, and stirs up strife, and incites men to litigation, and then he will sell his services as a lawyer to the highest bidder, without any regard to the rights of the case. "His pen," as the common proverb has it, "is sharper than a knife," and slays more fortunes, and murders more hopes, than the sword. And yet we must not be too hard upon him. His training morally has been a bad one. He has never seen a Bible, and he has no knowledge of a God. The word "sin" in the Christian sense is an unknown term to him. He is an agnostic, pure and simple, and is content to leave the great problems of life, that will force themselves upon his mind, unsolved. Heathenism has no moral power to make a man good. When a nation loses God, decadence in every direction is the immediate result, and of this China is a standing testimony.

It is now pleasant to turn away from this repulsive feature in the Chinese character to speak of some of the strong points in it. The Chinese are one of the imperial races of the world, and are yet destined to play a mighty part in the great drama of nations. Physically they are strong and robust. They can live and thrive in all kinds of climates, and under the most unhealthy conditions. A Chinaman will make a little straw hut, just big enough to creep into. He will then place it right down amongst the standing water in which his rice is growing, and he will sleep there for weeks, watching his crops till they are ripe and harvested. One night in that hut would be enough to give an Englishman such a dose of fever that it would take all his strength and all the skill of his doctor to bring him back to life again.

The Chinaman is as strong mentally as he is physically. His mind is of a broad common-sense type, and he has the solidity and the conservatism that are characteristic of the typical Englishman. There is one feature in which he is specially like him, and that is in the dogged, persevering way with which he holds on to his purpose. Nothing seems to be able to divert him from it. Difficulties may arise and obstacles intervene, but he will patiently bide his time, till, finally, after long waiting it may be, he gets his plan carried out. It is this heroic virtue that explains the marvellous growth of the Chinese empire, and the still more wonderful fact that the Chinese have not merely subdued surrounding nations, but also transformed them in language, and in national sentiment, till they have become one with themselves. Such is the terrible force and energy of this remarkable race, that they have always succeeded in absorbing those they have conquered, and in transmuting them in the course of time into Chinese. The same process has been effected with their conquerors. The Tartar armies, about the middle of the seventeenth century, invaded and conquered China. The fierce soldiers of Tartary have in time been subdued, yet no weapon has been seen in the struggle, no shock of arms, and no great and crowning victory, in which countless slain mark the place where fortune changed and the victor became the vanquished. It has been the victory of mind, and thought, and force of character. The supremacy has been gained by untiring perseverance and a determination that knows of no change of purpose. These are the forces that have turned the Tartars into Chinese, and made them one with the " Black-haired race." The Emperor, in times of emergency, may flee back to the home of his fathers, but the children of the men that conquered China will not follow him, for their homes are in the Middle Kingdom, and they have for ever thrown in their fortunes with the people of the land.

The Amoy people, amongst whom the missionaries came to preach the Gospel, are sturdy representatives of their race. They are heathen, be it remembered, and no more vivid and graphic picture of what this means has ever been given than that which an inspired hand has drawn in the first chapter of Romans. They are very fiery and passionate when any injustice or wrong is attempted, but generally they are fair-minded and amenable to reason. They have an Englishman's sense of fair play, and they have an intense respect for virtue and goodness of every kind, and they will pay devout homage to any one in whose lives these are conspicuous. The story of what the Gospel has done amongst them, in changing and transforming their lives, is not amongst the least marvellous and romantic of the missionary annals of the world.

CHAPTER III.

FIRST SUCCESSES.

THE London Missionary Society first occupied Amoy in the year 1844. The Rev. John Stronach, one of its missionaries, was ordered to remove from Singapore, where he had been labouring for some years, and take up his permanent residence in this place. In a few months he was joined by his brother, and for many years they were most suceessful preachers of the Gospel in Amoy and the region around.

Soon after his arrival, Mr. Stronach succeeded in renting a large building for religious services in one of the busiest and most crowded thoroughfares of the town. It was situated in Sack Street, so named because it was famous for the manufacture and sale of sacks. It is anything but picturesque. It is very narrow and dirty, and in wet weather very unsavoury and uninviting, and yet it was most admirably suited in those early days for the preaching of the Gospel. It was a most important thoroughfare. From early dawn till late at night a continuous stream of people passed with never-ending tread in it, for, though a short street, it was a main artery, which connected some very large ones in different directions around it, and to get directly to them, this had to be used.

All classes of people consequently travelled through

it. Rich merchants, in their costly silks, whose business places were situated a few streets off, near the seaside, took this road. Scholars in their long robes, with their keen, intellectual-looking faces, mingled with the crowd, for at the end of the street there were several famous book-shops, where all kinds of literature could be bought. Coolies, with great burdens, came panting and shouting along it. Mandarins in their luxurious sedan chairs, that almost filled up the street, crushed through the crowds on their way to visit some wealthy merchant friend. It was a busy, restless street, where the sounds of human life and the ceaseless tramp of men resounded the live-long day, and even far into the night.

No sooner were the doors of the building opened, than it was thronged with hearers, that crowded round the preacher, and listened as long as he had strength to go on. The congregation could never fail with such an incessant stream outside upon which to draw. The wonderful fact that an Englishman was addressing the people in their own language proved irresistibly attractive to all classes. After more than forty years the charm is still a powerful one, for the foreign missionary can always command an audience, whenever he stands up to preach the Gospel. But it was not simply curiosity that drew the crowds around the first preachers. The people were mightily stirred by the new method they adopted to make their Gospel known. It was one they had never seen before. The religious sects in China do not preach their doctrines promiscuously to the masses. They have no regular services which their adherents attend, and no class of men set apart

D

to preach the peculiar tenets of their faith. Neither the Confucian scholars nor the heathen priests ever dream of addressing popular assemblies for the purpose of inducing men to become believers in their systems. The only class of people to whom the missionaries could be likened were the public story-tellers, that are found in every town throughout the empire. At first, and indeed for many years afterwards, the popular name for the missionaries was "story-tellers," or more literally, "tellers of ancient things." These story-tellers gain their living by reading romances and historical novels in public. They generally choose the large vacant place in front of a temple. Here congregate pedlars of sweetmeats and eatables, as well as loafers and idlers, who find time hang heavily on their hands, and who are ready to be amused by these men. These story-tellers are mostly men of loose character, opium smokers, or men who have failed in life through their own folly. They are very highly appreciated, however, by certain classes of the community. Tradespeople, artisans, the jolly rollicking fellows whose aim is to get all the pleasure out of life possible, flock in crowds to hear them. Their stories have a wide range, and are taken out of every period of Chinese history. The great kings whose names are famous in the annals of their country, and the ilustrious statesmen whose genius has left its impress upon the laws and thoughts of the nation, are portrayed with wonderful vividness and power. The exciting scenes of past history, the great battles on which hung the fortunes of the empire, the stern and bloody conflicts, when Tartar or Mongol hordes invaded China and became the conquerors, to be ultimately lost and absorbed amongst the masses of the conquered, are all told to breathless and excited audiences.

When the first missionaries commenced their public work of preaching, the populace could only imagine that a new set of story-tellers had arisen. They were not long in discovering the vast difference there was between them and the men after whom they were named. This was a decided advantage, but still a vast amount of work had to be done before the populace could understand the divine truths that seem so simple to us, but which are mysterious and profound to a heathen mind. It is utterly inconceivable how difficult it is for such to grasp spiritual ideas. Idolatry seems to have the power of eliminating all such out of the mind, and of disqualifying it for reasoning about them. I hold a conversation, for example, with an extremely intelligent Chinaman. He is as keen and sharp as a needle in worldly matters. He is so shrewd a business man that in a moment his mind has grasped, even in its minutest details, some great transaction in which thousands of dollars are involved. I speak to this same man about some of the simplest truths of Christianity, and his intelligence seems at once to have vanished. I speak to him of God, a living personal Being, the Creator of the mountains around that are bathed in a great ocean of light, but there is a vacant look about his face as though he were trying to master a thought that was too great for him. His native politeness will make him nod his head in acquiescence of what I say, but I know he does not understand me. How should he? God as a Person, mingling in human life, and full of sympathy and compassion for man, of Him he knows nothing. The silent idols that he bows down before have never taught him of Him. The priests that burn the incense for him, and mutter certain forms of prayer by his side have never spoken to him of Him, for they are just as ignorant on this question as he is himself. No word about God has ever fallen from the lips of his parents during all the years of his childhood, and now the only man that can speak to him about Him is the Christian. It takes many conversations with such a man before he can take in the conception that is familiar to any ordinary intelligent boy in our Sunday-schools in Great Britain.

The early missionaries therefore had to do what has to be done in the establishing of mission work in every new place from that time to the present. They had to make it their business to saturate the people with Christian ideas, and to fill the very air with the music of the name of Jesus. They had to reveal to them a spiritual world, peopled with forms that reason could not disclose, and to get them to have thoughts about life and the future such as their greatest sages had never even hinted at. In addition to all this serious work, they had to defend themselves against the doubts and suspicions that ere long began to be entertained in regard to their own character and the purpose they had in coming to China. The Chinese do not believe in the existence of disinterested benevolence, and therefore they were certain the missionaries had other motives for their self-denial beyond those they publicly gave out. The most absurd and abominable stories got abroad in regard to them, and placards were posted on the walls and

AN OPIUM SMOKER.

circulated through the villages, warning the people against them. The opium question met them in a very objectionable form in the early years of their work. It was reported, and the rumour lives even to the present day in out-of-the-way places, that the missionaries took out the eyes of the Christians after death to make opium of them. This was believed in by every class of the community. The scholars accepted it as true; the commonest coolies repeated it; the middle classes everywhere talked about it as a fact, and even the mandarins were prejudiced against the Christians, because they believed the common report.

Four years thus passed away, and still no impression seemed to have been made upon the large numbers that during that time had listened to the preaching of the Gospel. Crowds had come, and crowds had gone, but they appeared utterly untouched. One would like to have got behind those stolid-looking faces, and have read their thoughts, as they sat so patiently and listened with such attention. The Story of the Cross, that has melted so many, seemed to have lost its virtue here. Has its ancient power vanished, or is it one that is suited only to the genius of the men of Western lands?

The year 1848 is a notable one in the history of the Amoy mission, for in it the missionaries had the unspeakable pleasure of baptizing two men, a father and his son, the former being over sixty years of age.

They were artificial flower-makers by trade, a branch of industry for which Amoy is famous. It would seem surprising that a man so old as the father was should have been willing to abandon beliefs that had grown up with him from his childhood for a new faith preached by foreigners. He was literally steeped in idolatry. According to human reasoning such a man will be the very last to feel the influence of the new faith. The experience of the missionary is in direct opposition to such a theory. Truth is imperious, and when it touches a man's heart, be he old or be he young, be he moral or immoral, he must yield. I have often been taught the folly of laying down rules by which I thought the Divine Spirit might operate. I have seen young men, with many excellent and amiable qualities, who seemed so close to the kingdom that they had to take but a single step and they would be inside, go back into heathen life and vanish completely from sight. I have known, on the other hand, men advanced in years, of the very lowest moral reputation, after a brief acquaintance with the Gospel, become sincere and humble disciples of the Lord Jesus.

The two individuals who were the first converts in our mission were simple, uneducated men. Their occupation being necessarily a sedentary one, they had ample opportunities for the quiet discussion of many subjects, that others of more active employments had not. Rumours had reached them that the missionaries had established themselves in their town, and were engaged in preaching strange doctrines such as neither they nor their forefathers had ever heard. Many a chat did they have as they sat pasting the many-coloured leaves together, and deftly fashioning the various kinds of flowers, that were soon to adorn the heads of women far and near. What could they be preaching about? It was not at all likely that the barbarians would come away from the western seas simply to amuse them as their own professional story-tellers did. They questioned their customers, or chatted with their neighbours after they had finished their evening meal of rice before they retired to bed. Opinions differed about these missionaries. Some thought they were good men, and that their only aim was to benefit the people. Others, of the sharper and shrewder kind, the knowing ones in fact, had a totally different estimate of them. They had discovered that behind all this pretended disinterestedness there were deep laid schemes for the ruin of their country. They had come, they said, from the lands in the western seas on purpose to teach the Chinese how to obtain happiness, but this story was manifestly untrue. What could the barbarians know of benevolence? They had never been enlightened by the teachings of the great sages of China. They reasoned thus: "We should never dream of making the sacrifices that these men do. It is quite inconceivable, indeed, that such ideas of self-sacrifice should ever originate with any one in the Central Kingdom, and if not in it, how much less amongst the barbarians, who have never felt the civilizing influences of the great Yau and Shun."

They pointed triumphantly to the opium traffic, and asked how a people that grew and sold opium could be moral or benevolent. Besides, was it not a tradition, graven deep into the heart of the nation by many a bitter experience in the history of the past, that the barbarian was ever the foe of China, whose lands and riches he coveted? Was it conceivable that his nature could ever change? Impossible! He was but changing his tactics. Instead of lance and spear, and wild and bloody inroads, he came as he pretended for purposes of trade, and to preach doctrines which he said would benefit the people, whilst he was really laying deep schemes, when he had won the affections of the people, for possessing the Empire for himself.

The old man at length determined to go and hear for himself. He entered the church with a good deal of curiosity. He found it pleasantly fitted up, with a number of forms all ready placed for the comfort of the listeners. He was pleased with the appearance of things, and especially with the urbanity of the missionary. The room in the meantime became filled with people, and the preacher in a solemn earnest way began to expound the very simplest truths of the Gospel. He spoke of God, not simply as one of the idols of the foreigners, but the Supreme Ruler over all lands, and the same that their forefathers in the golden age of Chinese history had worshipped. He told of His power and His love, and His care for all men, good and bad. The old man listened with open mouth. Never in all his life had he heard such wonderful doctrines as these. No romance that the story-tellers had ever told, or deed of daring, pictured in their most graphic and realistic manner, had ever touched his heart as these had done. He was full of the subject when he returned home, and he and his son discussed it, as they fashioned the leaves and petals of the flowers that seemed to grow like magic from amongst their fingers.

The father would have his son go with him the next time he went to listen to the missionary. Unconsciously to himself, he had become a believer in the truth. The more he heard, the more entranced he became. The preacher told him that God was not only omnipotent, but that He was also exceedingly willing to listen to, and deliver every man that called upon Him. This came to him as a mighty revelation. The idea of a personal God, mingling in human life, and full of love and concern for mankind, was one that was entirely new to him. Up to this time he had firmly believed in the idols, but many a time in his long life had he found them fail him. He remembered how in seasons of perplexity he had made his offerings to them, and prayed for their help. He had thrown the divining rods, and the answer they gave him through them was favourable. He had got assurances, too, from the idol mediums who were supposed to be specially inspired by the gods, that his prayers would be answered. By and by he found that he had been deceived. Idols, and mediums, and divining rods had all equally been at fault. It was no comfort to tell him that his fate was an unlucky one, and that the idols were powerless to control that. It simply revealed to him that they were subject to the same weaknesses that paralysed human life. Now the God that these missionaries spoke about was the very reverse of all this. He was great, He was omnipotent, He was infinitely compassionate and loving, and His tender mercies were over all His works. He discovered that He was the very Being that he had been unconsciously longing for all his life. He and his son abandoned their idolatry, and were the first converts that were received into the Church.

Not long after the reception of these two men, another person who has played a conspicuous part in the history of our Mission became a Christian. As his case is full of interest, I shall give a somewhat detailed account of it. He was a military officer, who had made for himself a good reputation, and had every prospect of rising to a very high position in the army. A short time before his conversion, he had been sent with a detachment of his men on board a war junk to assist in attacking some pirates that had been plundering the merchant vessels on the coast. In his conflict with them one of his eyes had been severely burnt by a "stink-pot." These stink-pots are favourite weapons with the pirates. They are filled with all sorts of combustible materials, and with some compound so terribly offensive, that when they explode they not only wound and burn, but also sweep the deck of every one that has any sense of smell. He had been invalided home until he could recover from his burns. Various Chinese doctors were called in to prescribe for him, but having no knowledge of surgery they could do nothing for him. The agony from his eye was excessive, so much so, that as he lay tossing about at night he devised a plan for committing suicide. An itinerant dealer in pork, who was accustomed in his daily rounds to serve the family, saw how severely the officer was suffering, and said to him: "I have heard that the English have opened a free hospital by the seaside, and they have invited all who are sick to go to it, and be healed. Some of my neighbours who have been ill have attended there and have been cured. They speak of the doctor as a man of great benevolence, and they praise his ability in healing the most desperate diseases. Why should not you go and be healed by him?"

The officer was profoundly indignant at this proposal. The mere suggestion that the barbarian doctors could do what the Chinese had failed in was perfectly abhorrent to his mind. "What!" he said, "do you wish to make me believe that the English doctors know more about medicine than ours? It is well known that China is the most enlightened country in the world. There is none that can be compared to it. I have consulted our own doctors and they have not been able to relieve me. It is not their want of skill that has caused them to fail, but it is because it is the will of Heaven that I should suffer. The barbarians cannot help me, and, moreover, I would rather die than submit to the disgrace of having anything to do with them."

A few more days passed by, but his sufferings continued to increase. His friends now urged him to visit the English doctor. At length worn out with pain, and careless of life, he started for the hospital. The reluctance with which he went, however, was manifest by the fact that he took the longest way round the town to get to it. At last he stood outside the door, his unwilling steps dragged there by the excruciating pain in his eye. He little dreamt that he had now approached a great crisis in his life, and that the kingdom of heaven had come nigh unto him. Let us look at him for a moment. He is a tall military-looking man, very solemn and dignified in his demeanour. He is a beau ideal Chinaman, whose brain is teeming with the traditions of more than three thousand years. To him there is no nation so great as China, and none whose history is filled with such splendid names. His inborn contempt for the foreigner is intensified by the thought that only a few years ago barbarian ships bombarded Amoy, and barbarian troops defeated the soldiers of the empire. Why, he can almost fancy as he looks on the hills around that he can hear the echo of the guns that made the soldiers fly before the fierce onslaught of the English. He is the last man in all this great city, one would suppose, that could be influenced by Christianity, and yet he is the one whom God has chosen to play a conspicuous part in the preaching of the Gospel in this region. The time has come, and workers are needed; for though foreign missionaries shall first tell the wondrous story of the Cross, it shall be Chinese hands that shall build up the Church in this land; and this Chinese soldier shall have the honour of laying the impress of his own great faith upon many who by his means shall be brought to believe in the Lord Jesus Christ.

As he entered the door, he found that a religious service was being held. The preacher was just giving out his text: "A good tree bringeth forth good fruit, and a corrupt tree bringeth forth evil fruit. A good tree cannot bring forth evil fruit, neither can a corrupt tree bring forth good fruit." He was startled by these words. He had been prepared for very strange revelations, in coming in contact with the foreigners. In the camp he had heard most outrageous stories of what the barbarians did and said, but here, on the very threshold of his acquaintance with them, he is arrested by a great and profound truth. He is bewildered, and he does not know what to think. He seats himself amongst the listeners, and as the preacher unfolds his subject, his heart is profoundly moved. Every word that he hears is true. This is very different from what he expected. This teaching is equal to anything that the sages of China ever uttered, and it evidently comes with more power, for how otherwise can he explain the wondrous impression it is making on his heart?

The service over, and his mind completely revolutionized in thought, he is taken before the doctor, who examines his eye. He is very pleasantly surprised by the appearance of this gentleman. Instead of a wild barbarian, with spear in hand, and fierce and savage mien, he sees before him a man so full of politeness, that he might have been trained in all the profuse etiquette of the Middle Kingdom. He told the officer that he must lance his eye, but that he could not give him any hope that he would ever be able to see with it again. The proposal to touch his eye with a lance rather staggered him. The Chinese have very peculiar ideas with regard to the various organs of the body, and how they ought to be treated. The free use of the surgeon's knife is a thing utterly unknown to the medical profession in China. It rather shook his faith in the doctor to find him advising that so delicate an organ as the eye should be touched with the knife. When I heard him say that my eye should be lanced, he has since told me, I was full of consternation. The eye, you know, he said, is a very soft tender thing, and by way of illustration he held up his right hand, with the fingers converging towards each other, as though he were gently and delicately holding the eyeball with them. A mere touch of the hand, and instantly it closes itself, and shrinks from it; but imagine a knife stuck into it! The consequences of such might be far reaching, and might even imperil the life. I told the doctor that what he proposed was so serious, that I must have some time to consider it.

He went home determined never to return to the hospital; but two or three days more of acute pain brought him back, prepared to submit to any operation, no matter what the risk might be. A slight incision gave him immediate relief, and after a series of visits to the hospital he was able to resume his duties, though the sight of his eye was gone for ever. His regular attendance at the hospital had given him the opportunity of becoming fully acquainted with the truths of the Gospel. These he listened to with intense delight. He attended every service both in it and in the church, and he was never wearied of listening to the story of Christ's love, as shown in His death on the cross for the sins of the world. Before many months had passed by he was received into the Christian Church by baptism.

When it became known that he was a Christian, he had to suffer a good deal of annoyance from his fellow officers. They could not comprehend how a gentleman and an officer could demean himself by even associating with the despised foreigners. Jokes and sneers were continually used to try and shake his faith. All the vile stories that were then beginning to circulate about them were repeated in his hearing. He was taunted with giving up his nationality, and in heart becoming a barbarian. These attacks did not for a moment influence him, excepting to drive him more to the company of the Christians and the missionaries. He now spent nearly all his spare time in the church, because he could then hear more of the truths that had become so precious to him, and also because he wished to take an active part in preaching them to his fellow-countrymen. The strong manly character of the man will be somewhat understood from the fact that he, an officer with brilliant prospects before him, had the courage to stand up before the crowds of heathen that daily flocked into the church, and preach a religion which was universally supposed to be merely a foreign sect, with which patriotic Chinese could have no possible concern.

On one occasion, at a united prayer-meeting of Christians and missionaries, this officer was asked to engage in prayer. There was a large crowd of heathen present as spectators, and amongst them some of the soldiers under his own command. These opened their eyes wide with astonishment when they saw one of their own officers taking a public part in this religious ceremony of the foreigners. On their return to the camp, they at once reported the matter to one of their officers, who made a formal complaint to the colonel. On the next day he sent an orderly to the officer, commanding him to appear at his quarters. When he entered his room, the commander, after addressing him in a very kind and polite manner, said: "I hear that you have become a member of the sect of the barbarians. Is that so?" The officer replied that he had been misinformed, for that such was not the case. "The fact of the matter is," he continued, "I have become a member of the Church of Jesus." "But how is it that such a promising officer as you are should have been so deluded as to give up your own beliefs, and adopt those of the men who are the enemies of China?" The officer then explained how he had been wounded in his engagement with the pirates; what agony he had endured, and how he had been treated by the foreign doctors. He also told him how he had been instructed in the knowledge of God, the very same God that their fathers in ancient times had worshipped; how as the character of God was revealed to him, his own sinfulness was impressed upon him, and how he had found in Jesus, the Saviour of the world, the true remedy for his distress of mind.

His superior officer listened to him very attentively, and then said: "If you want to be good and serve God, why not do so in your own home, or in your quarters here? There is no reason why you should be constantly associating with the foreigners, and thus bringing disgrace upon yourself and your regiment. Do you really believe that the Chinese don't know how to be good, and that you have to get this knowledge from these strangers?"

The officer replied that he was very sorry that he must appear insensible to the kindness of his superior, but he could not promise to do as he had advised him. "Very well, then," he said, "be sure that you are prompt and faithful in the discharge of your duties, for on the very first occasion on which you fail in any of them, I shall report you to the general, and have you dismissed from the army."

This man's faith was not a common one. He

must have had a profound conviction of the truth of Christianity to have thus disregarded the almost direct commands of his colonel. He had no influential friends to back him, for he was a poor man, and had come from a poor family. At present he was a rising man, and there was no reason why he should not attain to high position in the army, which in China invariably brings with it wealth and honour. Long years afterwards, indeed, one of his fellow officers, whose prospects were far less bright than his own, gradually rose in the army, and actually obtained the command of all the troops in the Amoy district. All these prospects he deliberately risked, rather than do anything that would interfere with his open profession of Christianity.

His faith was soon to be rewarded by a most signal deliverance from a great peril. On one occasion he was ordered out with an expedition in search of pirates, that had been committing depredations on the coast. The officer in command disliked Sok-tai because he was a Christian, and so he skilfully devised a scheme by which he felt sure he could ruin him. They had not been out to sea long, before the pirate junks were discovered in the distance. Chase was at once made, and as the wind was fair, and the gunboats were fast sailers, they soon began to overhaul them. The one that Sok-tai commanded was well in advance of the rest, and the breeze was so strong that he found himself fast getting up with one of the largest of the pirates. The commanding officer now determined to put into execution his plan for Sok-tai's destruction. He accordingly allowed his junk to get well ahead, until a considerable distance intervened between him and the rest of the squadron. As his vessel drew nearer the pirate, he discovered that she was too large for him to attack with any hope of success. Her decks were crowded with a crew of savage ruffians, who had forgotten what the word mercy meant, and who would fight to the bitter end rather than be captured. She was, indeed, already beginning to show fight, and the shot from her guns were whistling unpleasantly around. Sok-tai looked anxiously about for help from his consorts, but to his dismay he found that they were being purposely kept back. Whilst he was debating with himself what he should do, he saw the red flag hoisted on board the commanding officer's ship. This was an order for him to come to close quarters with the pirate and board her. He dared not disobey, for to do so would end in ruin to himself, whilst to carry out the command and attack such a crew of monsters, who were fighting for dear life, was attended with the greatest possible peril. He felt that there was none that could save him but God, and to Him he must appeal. Descending to his cabin, he knelt down, and cried: "O God, I am very weak. The enemy is in front of me, and the enemy is behind me. My only hope is in Thee. I know not what to do of myself. Deliver me, for the sake of Jesus Christ." Returning quickly to the deck, with his own hand he trained one of the largest of his guns against the pirate, when the shot carried away her tiller, and killed the helmsman. Immediately there was the greatest confusion on board. All control over the junk was lost, for there was nothing to steer her with, whilst the shot from the gunboat was making havoc amongst the pirates. A panic ensued, during which Sok-tai laid his junk alongside and boarded her. Some of the crew threw themselves into the sea, and were drowned; a large number were killed, and thirty-eight were taken alive, and subsequently beheaded.

After the action was over, Sok-tai went to make his report to the commander. When he appeared before him with the list of his prisoners, he found him standing on deck surrounded by his officers. As he drew near to him, he cried out, half in earnest, half in banter: "Your God certainly is the true God: to-day you owe your safety to Him." Sok-tai's heart was too full to reply. The thought of the great peril through which he had just passed, and the wonderful deliverance that God had given him, filled his mind, so he merely bowed and then retired.

The answer to his prayer that day was one of the turning points in his life. It was not simply that he had been delivered from the pirates. He had had a vision of the Unseen, which was to qualify him for the great life-work to which God was calling him. Eighteen years ago he and I went together to commence work in a new region, where men had never heard of God. The people were notoriously bad. Opium smoking, and gambling, and other vices that follow in their train were rampant. The Gospel was preached there, and its divine power touched the hearts of opium smokers and gamblers, and in time a church grew and multiplied under his teaching. What was the one great truth he was able to impress upon that church? It was the reality of God, and of the unseen world. There are some things that no language can tell. They have to be taught by a life. I remember seeing a sunset in the China Sea that I shall never forget. The sky in the west was covered with beautiful fleecy clouds that floated lazily before a gentle breeze. All at once they were filled with the rays of the setting sun, that painted on them the most marvellous scenes. One panorama had scarcely faded before another still more beautiful took its place. Pictures of life fashioned themselves on the clouds, so real that I could scarcely believe that in a few moments they would melt away and lose themselves in others. Exquisite colours flashed through the bank, behind which the sun was hiding, and flashes of gold, and then of purple, and then of blood-red, followed each other in rapid succession, till finally one great band of afterglow streamed across the heavens, and I found myself involuntarily looking round to see if there was not another sun rising in the east. No painter, though a genius, could ever put that wonderful scene on canvas. No great poet, though inspired, could ever sing so divinely that those changing clouds, and golden rays, and flashing colours should be seen as God's hand had painted them on that evening sky. Now Sok-tai had to preach truths which it takes even Christians long to fully believe. He had to tell of God, mingling in human life, planning for men, very human in His affections, listening to every cry of the heart to Him, and full of the intensest sympathy for all. How shall he get opium smokers and gamblers, who require to have the very word God explained to them, to understand this? His own life shall tell what human language cannot; and the unseen world, which opened its mysterious gates to him through the flash of the cannon and the tumult of deadly conflict, shall, through his profound faith in it, become a reality in their life.

A very marked feature in the Amoy work is the fact that persons specially qualified by faith and character to be leaders of men were raised up by God at various periods of its history. This is a striking fact, indeed, in God's government of His Church in all ages. When America was about to become a nation, He did not leave the shaping of its destinies to discoverers, and adventurers, and men half sailors half pirates. Men of better character than these were needed to mould the thought and culture of a great nation, and so the *Mayflower* carried her precious freight across the stormy Atlantic, and landed on Plymouth Rock the choicest forces that ever went to lay the foundation of a great empire. So it was in Amoy. God left nothing to accident, or to the mere desultory preaching of a few foreign missionaries. Men of profound faith were called to stand by their side from amongst the people of the land, and to them belongs the honour of whatever success has been achieved in that region. Amongst the figures that stand out prominently before my mind's eye, is that of a woman, the influence of whose life was far-reaching, and whose memory is still fragrant in the Church. She was a little, quiet, sweet-tempered woman, with apparently not very much force of character. A slight acquaintance with her, however, showed that she was possessed of a power that was all the more forcible because it was wielded in such a loving, gentle way.

She was originally a member of a religious sect called the "Vegetarians," because on religious grounds they were opposed to the taking of life in any form. She heard of the new doctrines that were being preached, and so she determined to go and hear what they were. She was deeply impressed, for there was a directness and a simplicity about them that contrasted favourably with those she had been accustomed to. The revelation of a personal God, and a Saviour who had redeemed her, came home with power to her soul. There was no need for her to ask for the evidences of their truth. The strongest proof was that they touched her as she never had been touched before. She went home with her mind in a state of bewilderment. She had not had time to think the subject out fully, and yet she was conscious that her life had been in some mysterious way changed by what she had heard. She felt her own beliefs slipping from her heart in spite of herself. There was one thing that had greatly perplexed her. She had been told that her abstinence from animal food was of no avail for the forgiveness of her sins, and she was advised to trust in Christ instead. This seemed to her horrible. For many long years she had denied herself many articles of food, in the conviction that she was accumulating such an amount of merit that she would by and by have assigned her a very high position in the "Western Heaven." Was the self-denial of all those years to count for nothing? She could not endure this thought, and she determined that whatever else she might give up, she would at least hold on to this part of her old faith. As she became better acquainted with Christianity, her views completely changed. She saw the folly of believing that the abstinence from any particular food could cleanse her soul from sin. She soon learned that the one royal road to purity was through the blood of Christ, and ere long she gave up her vegetarianism, and became a devoted follower of the Lord Jesus. For many years she had been in a delicate state of health, and had suffered greatly from weakness. After her reception into the Church, she seemed to get a new lease of life, and she enjoyed good health for many years afterwards.

Her conversion to Christianity had an immediate effect upon her own family. She was a weak, gentle-spirited woman, but with a good deal of quiet power that gave her great influence over others. She had several sons; sturdy fellows they were, too, and very independent in manner, but with boundless admiration for their mother. The eldest of them was a brusque, impulsive man, and very outspoken, as most of the Foh-kien men are. He seemed so unlike his mother, and yet her gentleness formed the unseen basis that lay behind his outer life, and which was yet to make him a power amongst men, after the Spirit of God had converted him. At the time she became a Christian, he was a leader amongst the idolaters. He had been elected for the year to look after the public services that were to be held in connection with the temple of his district. His duties were to see that the customary plays should be performed on the birthdays of the idols, and at the great festivals of the year. He was highly indignant that his mother should give up the religion of their fathers for that of the despised foreigner. He reasoned with her in his rough yet respectful way. The little woman allowed the great strong man to say all that he could in defence of the idols. There was a magnetic influence, however, about her very gentleness that touched him. She spoke, too, with such dignity of the new truths that had altered her own life, and given her absolute peace, that ere long he was silenced. He was a shrewd, practical man, and he could not but see the difference between the divine truths of the Gospel and the miserable lives and teachings of the priests. Before long he became an earnest seeker after the truth, and soon there was no more devoted follower of Jesus than he. The whole family in time became Christians, together with the sons' wives and their children. Although she and her husband have gone home years ago, her grand-children and great-grand-children now fill a large space in the church every Sunday as they assemble for worship.

And so the years went by, though they were not marked by any very great success. Preaching was carried on very regularly. Mr. Stronach made it a daily practice to preach in the streets, and in front of the great temples, and in prominent places of the town. As he was a thorough Chinese scholar, and had an intimate acquaintance with the books of Confucius, the scholars that came to discuss with him were constantly foiled by the weapons supplied by their great sage's writings, whilst at the same time they were told of truths that he had never revealed to them. Christian ideas were thus becoming more familiar to the people, who were gradually getting accustomed to the thought that a greater

Name than any of their most famous sages was being taught them by these foreign teachers. At last the year 1855 arrived, a famous one in the history of the mission, for in it no fewer than seventy-seven persons were received into the Church by baptism, whilst a considerable number in addition came under religious instruction, and professed themselves desirous of becoming Christians.

From this year may be dated the commencement of that marvellous work that has not only made its influence to be felt in Amoy, but which has also spread far away into the interior, and demonstrated its divine power in the formation of churches, many of which are to-day self-supporting.

CHAPTER IV.

CHIANG-CHIU.

THE year 1861 was an important one in the history of the Amoy Mission, for during it a house was obtained in the large city of Chiang-Chiu, from which missionary work could be carried on, and where a Church might be formed of such as believed. The Rev. W. K. Lea, who had joined the Mission in 1856, and had devoted a great deal of time to itinerating in the country districts, selected this place because it would be a most admirable centre from which to carry on the new work. The town is about twenty-five miles from Amoy, and at that time was estimated to contain at least one hundred and fifty thousand inhabitants. It is delightfully situated in the midst of a very extensive plain, which is bounded on nearly every side by hills and mountains. Two rivers flow through the opposite sides of it, and it is on the banks of one of these that the city has been built. The plain, for miles around, is dotted with innumerable villages, which have a thriving, well-to-do appearance. Nature has bountifully supplied all the people's wants. The rivers are a perpetual source of prosperity to them, for they rarely know what drought means. In other places, when the clouds withhold the rain, and the springs are dried up, and the fiery Eastern sun pours down his fierce rays, blasting and scorching the crops in the fields, the farmers there look on with aching hearts, for they well know that this means sorrow and suffering to themselves and their families. Here they are almost independent of rain, for the rivers are at hand, and their waters, trained with skilful and patient hands, find their way throughout the plain, and into far-off and out-of-the-way places, and cover them with luxuriance and beauty.

A sail up the Chiang-Chiu River during any of the summer months, though trying, is a very delightful one. The great sun pours down his light in continuous billows, as if in the very wantonness of his power, and flashes his rays upon fields of waving rice, and paints, with exquisite colours, mighty creepers, that twine and twist over mouldy walls and sides of houses and round the stems of trees, with their purple cups looking straight up into his face, as they quaff great draughts of sunshine. Here, close by, is an immense banyan tree, that the forefathers of the village planted more than two hundred years ago. Its huge boughs stretch far out from the stem, and branches innumerable, with fadeless leaves, make a dense covering that no sun can penetrate. Among its gnarled and rugged roots that project far above the ground, stone seats have been fixed, and we can see a slab hoary with moss and lichen, that the men and women that have lain sleeping on the hill-side for many a long year used to sit on, but which the growing roots have caught within their embrace, and claimed as their own for ever. A little farther on is a clump of bamboo trees. How graceful they look with their long tapering stems and feathery leaves, and with what ease and grace they bend and bow before the breeze that comes up the river! They are the poetry and the romance in the landscape, for though there are other trees that are grander and more magnificent, there is none whose history and life is so entwined with those of the people as the bamboo. The ancient history of China, with its story of conquest and fierce conflict with barbarian invaders, who were tempted by the richness of the country, were first recorded upon it. The poetry of the past, the lives of the great, the struggles of the poor to-day for very life, and the luxuries of the great, are all associated with the elegant trees that bend in exquisite unison before the breeze that sends the junks flying up the river.

The scene on the river is always a lively one. As it is the great highway to the city, boats of all descriptions are continually passing up and down. Great boats filled with all kinds of merchandise from Amoy, with enormous latteen sails, dash by, under the influence of the strong monsoon wind. Passenger boats crowded with their fares come close up to us, and the people that are sitting closely packed together, look keenly and wonderingly at us, while the almond-shaped eyes twinkle with mirth as some one in a low voice makes some funny remark about us or our appearance. But see! here is a huge, unshapely-looking craft coming down against the wind, but with the tide in its favour. It is a boat that is specially characteristic of this river, and plies between Chiang-Chiu and Amoy. It has a very tall mast and a huge heavy sail, and it is housed in with strongly made bamboo mats, which serve the double purpose of protecting the family that lives in it, and the cargo from the weather. She is now being propelled by half a dozen sturdy rowers, the most of them being women. These latter can handle a boat just as well as the men. They can pull an oar, or hoist the sail, or steer the boat with the best of them. As we swing by her with the strong breeze behind us, we have a passing glimpse of the family life on board. The sons with their wives are busy at the oars, straining every nerve to keep her on her course. One of the younger women with a baby strapped on her back, has charge of the tiller, whilst at the same time she does her work at the rowing; and it is interesting to watch how deftly she moves it, and with what apparent unconcern she steers her way amongst the crowd of boats that thread their course in and out amongst each other, as though they were instinct with life.

Just in front of the rowers, in the stern, several children are running about, who find the old grandmother a delightful centre around which to gather. She has one of the youngest in her lap, which has twinkling black eyes and a closely shaven head, and is laughing and crowing, just as babies do all over the world. The grandfather is busily engaged over a huge pot of rice, which sends out bubbles of steam, and plainly intimates that they had better haul up to the bank, and anchor for a while, for the dinner hour is at hand. It is a pleasant, homely sight, and we have here an insight into the kind of life that the water population on this river lead. This boat is the only home they know. Their lives are spent in it. The man brings home his wife here, and the bride is welcomed with furious beating of gongs, and uproarious noise of fire crackers from the neighbouring boats. Sons and daughters are in course of time born on the boat; and when these have grown up, the girls are married from it, whilst the sons bring in their wives to add to the family circle. When life is at length ended, the offerings to the dead are spread in front of the coffin, and the priest chants his service in the very place where the dead has spent his life, and the body leaves it direct for the grave on the hill-side amidst the sounds of lamentation, and the loud explosion of fire crackers.

When I first visited the city, the approaches to it were very fine. As is usual in China, it was surrounded by a high wall, in which were four gates that corresponded with the four cardinal points. On the south side it was flanked by the river. A main street ran alongside this, and it was one of the busiest in the whole town, for here were congregated goods of all descriptions, that had been brought from the coast and the inland towns by the boats that lay anchored in the stream. It was a crowded, busy thoroughfare, and men from early dawn till late at night were absorbed in business. The street leading to the east gate, however, was by far the finest, for it was the great highway along which people travelled who were going north or south. Mandarins on public business, or going to their posts, carried in luxurious sedan chairs, and attended by crowds of attendants, had to pass along it. Couriers, from the far distant capital Peking, bustled along with ostentatious haste bearing despatches from the Dragon throne. Coolies with heavy burdens that they had carried for many weary days, with perspiration streaming down their bodies, and with hot and jaded-looking faces, staggered along it. It was a street where at times every phase of life, and representatives of nearly every province, could be met with, and a really magnificent one it was. It was ornamented for a mile and more with scores of beautiful stone arches, that had been erected by imperial permission in commemoration of the conspicuous virtues of certain of the citizens of this region. The general design of these was the same, but considerable latitude had been shown in the details. They stood fifteen or twenty feet high, and spanned the road. The inscriptions could thus be seen by every one, and thousands every day could read about sons that had been pre-eminent for their filial piety, and of widows that had elected never to marry again, and who for a long life had illustrated the homely virtues by their modesty, and the fidelity with which they had trained their children to be good citizens of the empire. The city itself, when viewed from the walls, was one of the most beautiful that I have ever seen in China. Looking over it, it seemed like one huge forest. The Chinese have a passionate love for trees and flowers, and consequently every householder had planted some kind of a tree in his courtyard. These, during years of undisturbed prosperity, had grown large and spreading, until at length the city seemed to lie beneath the shadow of a mighty forest. Lines of streets could here and there be distinguished through the foliage, but it was difficult to realize that down below, a hundred thousand people lived, that great busy streets, crowded with buyers and sellers, stretched far away into the distance, or that the river beyond was lined with craft of all kinds, in which thousands of people passed their lives, and had no home besides them.

The people of Chiang-Chiu were proud and haughty. They were prosperous and well-to-do. The great plains around them produced enough food for the city, and still they could afford to export large quantities of rice to Amoy. This was a famous kind. It was the whitest in all the region, and could always command a good price. They were proud, too, because of the exquisite silks and satin stuffs they could produce. Their looms were famous, and their designs were rare, and beautifully executed. They had the most supreme contempt for foreigners, and showed it in a very unpleasant manner. It was always unpleasant, and sometimes even risky, to travel about the streets in the day time. In certain parts of the town, such as the city gates, or the open spaces in front of the temples, where crowds of idlers were wont to assemble, one was always sure of being instantly surrounded by a mob, that seemed to be boiling over with delight at the idea of getting some fun out of the foreigner. In consequence of this haughty, overbearing spirit, mission work was carried on with extreme difficulty. Crowds of people would come into the church, which was opened daily for preaching, simply to have a look at the foreigner, just as men might gather to see a menagerie, or some strange grotesque sight. A group of young bloods, for example, would come swaggering in. They would be invited in our politest Chinese to be seated. They would stare at us with a look of the most profound contempt, and then break out into noisy conversation,

A CHINESE JUNK.

walking about and examining everything that struck their fancy.

They were once more invited to sit down, and have some tea, for in accordance with Chinese etiquette, we had a tea-pot and half a dozen tiny cups, that would hold about three or four thimblefuls each, always ready, to carry out the hospitable ideas that prevail throughout Chinese society. They would rudely decline, and by and by stalk out with some insulting expression at the impudence of the barbarians daring to come to their city to teach them.

Whilst these young fellows were acting in this offensive manner, a number of shopkeepers would come in, and although these did not dare to take the same liberties that the others did, there was still the same scornful look about their faces. They, too, were invited to be seated and partake of some tea. One or two of the better disposed would do so, but the rest would simply shake their heads and refuse. We then began to talk to them about God, and about Christ, who gave His life for the world. We spoke to them of God as a living person, who cares for every human being, and whose love for all no human language can express. These were new thoughts to our audience. In all their life they had never heard such before. Their only conceptions of Him had been taken from the idols, and these had never spoken to them of love, or of anxiety for the welfare of mankind. As we continued our discourse, the contemptuous look on their faces began gradually to melt down into one of surprised attention, and when they bid us good-bye it was with much kindlier feelings than when they entered.

Those early days were exceedingly trying ones. We had to carry on our work with the knowledge that the sympathies of the people were decidedly against us. The great mass of the population knew absolutely nothing of what Christianity was. It was something that was preached by the despised foreigner, and that was enough to condemn it. We had simply to be patient, and preach and preach until the Gospel should tell its own story, and win its own way into the hearts and consciences of men. It was only the eloquence of the tale it had to tell, and its own native power to touch the heart, that could bring this people to Christ.

It was intensely interesting to watch the process by which this was accomplished. One man I have a very vivid recollection of. He was a doctor. He was a very fine, handsome-looking man, and when at his ease he had a dignified bearing that gave him the appearance of being a man of power. If his mind had corresponded to his body he would have been, but unfortunately it did not. He was of a nervous, timid disposition, and seemed to be perpetually on his guard lest he should do or say anything that would compromise him with his neighbours. He came into the church one day, and was at once arrested by the wonderful truths that he heard. After this he was an almost daily visitor at the church, and became an earnest seeker after the truth. There was one thing about him that we disliked, and that was his want of courage to confess Christ. He always seemed to live under a perpetual dread lest he should be recognised by any in his visits to us. At first he used to come late in the evening, when there were few people in the street, and it was too dark for him to be known by the passers-by. When he left us, he would first open the door very cautiously, peer hastily into the darkness, and not hearing any footsteps, would plunge hastily into the street, and go off at railway speed for a few yards, until he was far enough off from the church not to be suspected of having come from it. After a time, as he became more fully instructed in the truth, he grew more bold, and finally agreed to attend our Sunday services. It was amusing to watch his conduct for some months after he had consented to take this public step. When the doors were opened for the service, the heathen as usual soon began to crowd in. Our doctor took good care not to seat himself too near the Christians, lest he should be identified with them, so he sat a little apart by himself. When the singing was commenced, though he held a hymnbook in his hand, he acted his part so well, that the heathen would never dream that he was anything more than an interested spectator, and anxious merely to know what these Christians were singing. By and by, when the people stood up to pray, he made it a point of keeping his eyes wide open, and moving his head about as though he was absorbed in the study of every article of furniture in the room. When he was spoken to about this, he would reply in a low, mysterious tone of voice: "Ah! you don't know the difficulty in which I am placed. Were my patients to find out that I was a Christian, they would all dismiss me, and then what should I do? Besides, you don't know what a temper my wife has got, and what a life she would lead me, if she got to know that I came here. Let me go on by degrees, and God will help me to confess Him more boldly as I get more faith and trust in Him.

In the course of time he lost a good deal of his timidity, and gave up the farce of trying to make the heathen believe that he was nothing more than a curious listener. He joined heartily in our services, though he still exhibited such nervousness and timidity that we could not be quite so proud of him as we should otherwise have been. This was constitutional, however, so we had to be patient with him. After he had been fully instructed in the Christian religion, and had given us satisfactory evidence of his sincerity, we proposed to him that he should be baptized. This he was firm in declining. With a shake of the head, and a solemnly mysterious look about his face, he said: "There is something in my home that has to be rectified before I can feel worthy of baptism." We asked him what it was, but he only became more sphinx-like in his answers. Our curiosity was aroused. It must surely be something terrible since he refused to give us even a hint of what the family skeleton that troubled his conscience so was. We naturally became all the more anxious to find it out, but that solemn face and mysterious shake of the head gave us no clue. This went on for two years, but we never could get any nearer to the solution of the secret. At last it was revealed to us in the midst of a tremendous tragedy. The long-haired rebels made a sudden incursion into the city, captured it, and made an indiscriminate slaughter of the people. All that could escape through the city gates hurried away for dear life from the doomed town. Amongst these were the doctor, with his wife and little son. Soon after emerging from the east gate, they were met by a body of the rebels, who attacked the husband, and left him for dead upon the ground. The wife rushed on frantic with fear, and heart breaking with sorrow for the loss of her husband. At last she stopped in the middle of the road. Her belief in the idols, which had been intense until that day, was shattered. Nevermore as long as she lived was she to trust in them again. She knelt down under the great stone arches that I have described, and made a vow to the God of her husband, that if He would only deliver her and her son from death that day, she would serve Him only. She cared not for the crowds that were rushing distractedly by her, nor for the fierce bands that might be in pursuit. She was communing with God for the first time in all her life, and she could think of none else. Whilst she was thus engaged, her husband, who had only been stunned, came rushing along. When he saw his wife kneeling in the street, he was thunderstruck. "What are you doing?" he hurriedly asked her. "I am praying to God," she said; "I was so sad. I thought you were dead. My heart was breaking, and so I was beseeching your God to deliver me and my son." All the time she was speaking the doctor's heart was filled with rapture. Ever since he had been an open worshipper of God, she had been a most bitter opponent of Christianity. His home had been made most wretched. The idols had still been retained in the house by her, and it was these that had kept him back from baptism, for he felt it would be inconsistent for him to receive it whilst those were still worshipped in his home. He had kept all this a secret from us, because he had been loyal to his wife. A great load was at once lifted from his heart. It seemed nothing to him now that his home was in the hands of the rebels, that his means of subsistence were gone, and that he was a fugitive with possible death still before him. It was enough for him to know that his wife had made a solemn vow to the Lord to be His. "It is all right now," he said joyfully. "The Lord will hear you, of course. He has promised to answer prayer, and now we shall be a happy family indeed." His heart was filled with a supreme joy that excluded every other thought from it. Screams of affrighted women and children filled the air, but he heard them not. The tread of men rushing in terror from the city resounded around him, but he was absorbed in the one glad thought that his wife would now be a worshipper of God with him. The whole family managed to escape to Amoy. In time they were all baptized, and for many years were members of the church in Chiang-Chiu.

There is no more beautiful study for the missionary than to watch the silent process by which the Gospel wins its way in any community in spite of the fiercest opposition, and converts its bitterest opponents into its staunchest adherents. To stand up in the streets and preach the Gospel in those early years was an ordeal that the missionary of to-day knows nothing about. The preacher had no sooner taken up a position in some prominent place, than he was at once surrounded by a great crowd. The elements of which it was composed were very mixed. The loungers and idlers, whose time hung heavy on their hands, were promptly there, as there was some prospect of diversion. Some of these were rough, coarse fellows, ready for any kind of fun that might turn up. Coolies, with their huge burdens which they laid down in a convenient place where they could keep a watchful eye upon them, drew near. Scholars with their cynical looks, and undisguised scorn of the barbarian, stood by in their long gowns to hear what the preacher had to say that could be better than what their great sage Confucius had taught more than two thousand years ago. The crowd was entirely unsympathetic. There was not a single tie that bound them and the speaker together. There was a babel of voices, and very uncomplimentary expressions could be heard above the din. Young fellows were laughing and jeering in coarse language. The first thing to be done was to get the crowd not only quiet, but also into a good humour. In order to this, great patience was required, as well as a little humour, and a considerable amount of tact. A cross word or an impatient look would have delighted the crowd, whilst at the same time it would have prevented the preacher from getting any hold upon them for that day. Whatever the clamour and commotion around him, he must be calm. Whilst he is debating with himself how he shall begin his address, he notices on the doorposts of the house across the street two sentences written in a large bold hand. The one on the right says: "Life is like a dream before the awaking in the early morn." The other on the left declares that, "Life is like a game of chess: how the pieces shall be moved, no man can foretel." He instantly takes these as his text, and pointing the crowd to them, he endeavours to show them that there can be no true solution of the mysteries of life without a knowledge of God, and no escape from its sorrows and perplexities excepting through Christ, the Saviour of the world. The quotation of these inscriptions at once arrests the attention of the crowd. What! the barbarian has actually studied their books, and knows how to read their mysterious hieroglyphics. He is decidedly a better man than they thought him to be. They are hushed whilst he goes on speaking of the great Father, who with loving heart cares for mankind, and would shape their lives, and make them full of happiness, but they refuse to let Him. Incidents from life are taken, stories from their past histories, the comedies and tragedies of their own every-day life are woven into the story, and ere long the crowd are silent listeners, and they forget for the moment that they are being taught by a barbarian, for the Divine power of this new Gospel is holding them within its grasp. The scorn on the faces of the scholars is still there, but it is not so bitter. The pale opium smokers' faces around look sad and ghastly, as the preacher tells how Christ delivers men from all vices, and makes them good and happy citizens. At this point, he hears a man that is standing near him remark to another: "Why, this religion is not so bad as it is commonly reported to be. I have not heard him say a single thing that I can condemn. Every word is true." His companion nods his head, and replies: "That is indeed so." At last the preacher ends. The spell of his voice ceases. The old instincts of the crowd assert themselves, and soon the silent attention is changed into the turmoil and confusion with which he began. He seems to have effected absolutely nothing, and in the end not to have touched a single heart. But this is not so. The crowd has gone home with new thoughts. The shopkeepers who stood and listened will discuss in their homes the points that have been pressed upon them by the preacher. Their ideas about idolatry will never again be precisely what they were before, for besides the grim idol that has been to them the only power they knew, there has now come, dimly and shadowy it is true, the picture of Another, who may in time become the very light of their life. The great city was thus being educated in Christian truths, and to-day the audiences gather round the missionaries in quiet respectful attention, because the preachers in those early days, amidst noisy crowds and unsympathetic hearts, patiently and in faith preached a gospel that men now generally recognise to be true.

As the years went by, the Church at Chiang-Chiu gradually grew in numbers, till in 1865 the city was captured by the famous Tai-ping rebels, and utterly destroyed. Its people were murdered by thousands, its trees were cut down, and large portions of the town were left desolate and tenantless. Fortunately nearly all the Christians managed to escape to Amoy. After the city was recaptured by the Imperial troops, the inhabitants who had escaped flocked to their ruined homes. With the indomitable pluck and determination of the Chinese, they at once began to rebuild their city, and ere long streets sprang up, as if by magic, on the place where only heaps of broken bricks and rubbish lay before. The quarter where our old church had been was one wilderness of ruins, so that it was difficult to point out the place it once occupied. We had no desire, however, to go back to that neighbourhood, as its situation was not central or commanding enough. After a good deal of patient waiting, we were fortunate in being able to secure a house in the large thoroughfare just outside the east gate of the city. The people had been so thoroughly humbled by the awful disasters that had come upon them, that we were allowed to take possession without any molestation from any one.

When we began work afresh, we found the tone and temper of the people entirely different from what they had been before. The men were not so arrogant, and consequently they were less unruly in our public gatherings. Their enthusiasm for their idols, too, was greatly diminished. In the time of their peril, these either would not or could not deliver them, and so from either point of view, they had good cause for feeling somewhat coldly towards them. For several years we had marked success. Our numbers grew so large, that the building became too small for our Sunday services. We therefore purchased a piece of ground in a very prominent part of the same street, and there we erected a spacious church that has ever since been a conspicuous feature in it. In the meantime, before this, our work had so far prospered, that we determined to extend our operations into the country around. We accordingly rented a house in a busy market town some three miles away from the city, named "Bridge Head Market." The chief attraction of this place was that it was a large centre for business. On the fair days, which were frequent, the farmers from the villages far and near, and buyers from distant districts, assembled there for purposes of trade. The scene on these days was an exceedingly interesting one. The produce of the region was displayed in the open spaces, and crowds gathered, and voices were heard in noisy disputation about prices, and sounds of laughter, too, as jokes were cracked by some of the more facetious. All the while, the goods were rapidly changing hands, and were being carried away, some in boats, and some on the shoulders of sturdy fellows, that panted and perspired under their huge loads. The goods were of a very varied description. Here were large bags of rice full to repletion, and revelling as it were in the very luxuriance of their abundance. How white the grains are, and how large too! None such ever grow beyond the mountains that bound this plain. The epicure's eyes sparkle as he gazes with loving looks at the great bags so temptingly displayed. Red sweet potatoes, piled up in heaps, and deftly arranged in baskets, were laid out for the inspection of purchasers. They are the mealiest and the sweetest that can be got, and come from a certain district only, where the soil is suitable for the growth of such. Numberless jars of sugar, black as it was crushed from the canes, that grow so luxuriantly on this hot plain, were exposed for sale, to be carried away and refined, and shipped to far-off places in China. But what shall I say about the fruits? How abundant and beautiful they were, according to the time of the year! Great clusters of nai-tsi, bunches of plantains, baskets of peaches, oranges in the richest profusion from the orange-groves a few miles away; mangos plucked from the trees around, and pumelos in such abundance from the gardens at the foot of the mountains out yonder, that they were sold in the distant markets of Shanghai, and were shipped also to southern ports in China by the regular steamers.

Our church was situated close to the busiest part of the fair. Crowds flocked to hear the Gospel who had never heard it before. Farmers and farm labourers, with open mouths, listened to the truths that came to them, with as veritable a revelation as did any that was ever revealed in ancient times to the greatest of God's prophets. They had looked since childhood upon that great plain clothed twice a year in the beauty of waving fields of rice. They had watched the circle of mountains in the distance, in all the varying moods of that Eastern climate. Sometimes they were bathed in a great ocean of sunshine, sometimes they flashed and darkened with alternate lights and shadows, and again they were crowned with dense masses of clouds that clung to them as if in mortal dread of the driving gale; but never till the preacher told them had they ever dreamt whose hand had made them, or whose thought had clothed the world in such matchless beauty. Gamblers, with the hungry look in their eyes, and a slovenly uneasy gait, which the consciousness of the disrepute in which they were held by the public had given them, stood spellbound as they listened to the Divine teaching of Christ. Prodigals were arrested by the marvellous picture of themselves that He had portrayed ages ago. Others again, with keen and worldly faces, but out of which all spirituality had been obliterated by heathenism, listened with a grim smile of incredulity. Life was to them the only reality, and trade and money making, and the accumulating of wealth the only things about which a man ought seriously to concern himself. "The unseen world," they said, "was a mystery that no man had ever penetrated, and then come back to tell its story Why, then, trouble one's head about a matter that men could never know absolutely?"

And thus the Gospel was preached amongst all classes, and ere long we saw gathering around us those that were attracted by its great truths. Among the first was a person whose belief in Christianity brought almost immediate suffering to himself and family. He was a man of a good deal of character, though one would not have thought so from a passing acquaintance with him. His face had a gentle, almost feminine look about it, and there was a shy, reserved manner about him that seemed to indicate a lack of power to grapple with any question that demanded nerve or pluck. Behind that gentle face, however, there was a reserve of force that enabled the man, when the time came, to perform the most heroic deeds. His business was to examine the dollars that were given in payment during the progress of the fair, and ascertain whether they were good, and of sufficient weight or not. Farmers, when they had sold their produce, came to him with the purchasers, and had their dollars weighed and tested before they accepted them. He was known for his ability in detecting the counterfeit ones, no matter how perfect the imitation, and his reputation had spread, so that large numbers of farmers regularly employed him. Unfortunately some of these fair days fell upon the Sunday. A serious question now arose for decision. How was he to act on those days? Was he still to carry on his business as usual, or was he to close his shop, and refuse to examine the dollars of his patrons? To do the latter would imperil his business. We strongly urged him to keep holy the Sabbath day. He then explained to us how dependent he was upon his employment, and how the loss of that would bring poverty upon his family. We still adhered to our advice, and showed him, that now he had a new Power in his life, who had promised to honour those who honoured Him. After some time of hesitation, in which he was thinking out the question, he decided to give up all Sunday work, no matter what might be the consequences. The farmers came round as they had done for years with their dollars, and they could not understand why his shop was closed. They brought rolls of them to be examined, and they were amazed when he would not look at them. It was Sunday, he said. Sunday! what was the meaning of that? They had never heard the term before. They remonstrated with him, and threatened that they would give their custom to some one else. He remained firm; but before many months had passed, the bulk of his customers had left him, and he had to face the problem how he should provide for the needs of his family. He never faltered in his faith in God, nor though severely tried did he regret the sacrifice he had made. Many years have passed by since then, and he has proved by experience the faithfulness and loving-kindness of God to those who honour His law and keep His commandments. For many years there has been a church in Bridge Head Market, and many noble men and women have testified both by their life and by their death their faith in Christ as their Saviour.

The changes that have taken place during the thirty years of missionary work in this region are perfectly marvellous. On the 30th of June, 1859, Mr. Lea writes: "I have paid repeated visits to Chiang-Chiu. Several attempts have been made at various times to introduce the Gospel there, but owing to the opposition both of mandarins and people, with no apparent result. At the time of the (local) rebellion two native converts were preaching in the city. One was beheaded, and the other made his escape with difficulty. Ever since that time the visits of foreigners, and indeed of native Christians too, have been regarded with suspicion, and identified with insurrectionary movements. I cannot say that there is as yet more than a readiness to hear on the part of the people generally, but this, as contrasted with the unfriendliness and open opposition of former years, gives much room for encouragement. I only regret that all efforts, both on my own part, and on that of the friendly disposed residents to obtain a house for regular preaching have as yet entirely failed. A short time ago a young man, who had been a student. with a brother missionary at Amoy, returned to his home at Chiang-Chiu, and commenced meetings in his own house. In a few days he was arrested by an officer, reproved, and ultimately beaten by the mandarin."

These words read like a passage taken out of some

ancient history. Christianity is now an important factor in the place, and is recognised both by the people and the mandarins. To-day there is the widest liberty to preach the Gospel in the city and its large and influential suburbs, and men are free to become Christians, without the serious penalties of early days. Chiang-Chiu is now the seat of a separate mission. A large hospital has been opened, and thousands yearly are being treated. When these people return to their homes, it will be with new thoughts of Him who commanded His disciples not only to preach, but also to heal the sick; and they will tell the story of Him, that they have learned in the hospital, to friends, whose hearts will be melted when they think of Him through the lives of dear ones who have been restored to them in health and strength.

CHAPTER V.

KOAN-KHAU.

THE year 1861 was also an eventful one in the annals of mission work in the Amoy region. In the town of Amoy itself, the successes had been great beyond all expectation. The little church had grown so rapidly, and its numbers become so great, that it was in serious contemplation to build another church in a different part of the town, where many of its members resided. This would not only suit the convenience of the Christians in that neighbourhood, but would also form another centre from which active work could be carried on. This plan was actually carried out in 1862. In addition to the church in Amoy, two mission stations had been opened in villages near the town, and the populous city of Chiang-Chiu was occupied, and regular services were being held in a building, which, after years of waiting, had been secured in the very heart of the town. And now another step forward was taken, and a house was secured in the large market town of Koan-Khau, which lies some eight or nine miles to the west of Amoy. The position of this place made it a most admirable centre for missionary work. It was situated in the midst of a large farming population, that necessarily had constant communication with it, and could thus be easily reached by the missionary from it. The town is very picturesquely situated; it is built on a hill about two miles from the sea, and from it can be seen the numerous villages that cover the plain up to the foot of the distant mountains. Close behind the town there rises a splendid range of mountains, the highest in all that region, and the source of never-ending and varying beauty. It would seem as though nature were continually spending her highest and finest thoughts in designing the scenes she paints upon them. At one time they are covered with dense masses of clouds that hide them completely from view; again, they are bathed in golden sunshine that makes them stand out from the populous plain, one mass of glorious light, and again the fleecy mist floats along their sides over dark shadows and sunlit spots till it is lost in the morning sun.

With some little difficulty a house was rented, which was soon transformed into a church. Though it was a miserable place, we were very glad to get it. The main room faced the street, and was about twelve feet square. Here we had our pulpit, and the benches on which our future hearers were to sit; immediately above this was a room about half its size. This was reached by narrow stairs so steep that there was a risk to one's neck every time one came down them; for having no banisters, the only thing one had to hold on to was a rope that hung dangling from a beam in the roof. This was our sleeping room, dining-room, and reception room. Immediately behind the main room was a little dark den where any women that might be interested in the Gospel could sit; for it was entirely opposed to

Chinese custom to have the men and women sit together during a service. This room was lighted by a passage that led to a small courtyard where the kitchen was. It was a dismal place, and in the hot weather perfectly stifling, as not a breath of air could by any possibility get to it. In fact, the whole place was hot, and it was only by a vigorous use of the fan, that one could just manage to exist. In almost every place where we first go to, these initial difficulties have to be encountered. In time, when we have gained the confidence of the people, we can always rent better and more suitable houses. The congregations of some of our elegantly appointed churches in England would be astonished could they see the miserable houses in which their brethren and sisters sometimes have to worship God in China. Indeed, it would be a wonderful and romantic story that could be told of the wretched places in which the Church that is destined in the future to cover the land with beautiful buildings had its birthplace. Christianity has built magnificent churches and stately cathedrals throughout the world, but it must be remembered that the birthplace of them all was the stable in Bethlehem.

No sooner was the building opened for daily preaching than the people began to crowd in to listen to us. Men wanted to hear for themselves what we had to say. People had been to Amoy, and they had brought back rumours that the foreigners were preaching strange doctrines, such as their fathers had never listened to. They were greatly divided in their opinion about them. Some said they were good; others declared that they were abominable, and would upset the whole of the beliefs in which they had been trained. Now they could hear for themselves, and so men of all classes thronged around the door, and filled the place till it was quite packed, eager to hear what was said, but especially to see the foreigner, and to verify for themselves whether he was human or not, or whether in a strictly Darwinian sense he was descended from a monkey, and still retained enough of that animal to indicate his origin. Young country bumpkins with mouths wide open would stand and gaze, thunderstruck as they looked for the first time upon the barbarian. His dress was so different from their own, and his skin so fair; his head, too, was covered with a confused mass of hair, so unlike their own shaven heads, and queues neatly plaited. And then, wonder of wonders! this strange-looking being could really speak in Chinese, and not only so, but actually in the very patois that was spoken by themselves. They were transfixed. The missionary addresses a few words to them. They start back with amazement, and look around with a startled air, as though something was going to happen to them. He advances a little nearer to them in order to try and make them feel a little more at home, and they hastily retreat. It is some time before he can get them to be seated. Even when they are, they sit upon the edge of the bench, as though that was the safest position they could occupy under the circumstances. Old men with dry and wrinkled faces quietly sit down and listen by the hour to the doctrines that are being preached. They are village elders, and for many a year they have exercised a controlling influence in their villages; and as they generally belong to families that are strong in numbers, they have always the power ready at hand to enforce their decisions. Their faces have a stolid, unimpassioned look, and they have such wonderful command over themselves, that they can completely conceal their thoughts from us. They may be pleased or not, we cannot tell, for not a muscle in their faces indicates to us what effect our preaching is having upon them. The probability is they are intensely prejudiced against us, because the elementary truths we are preaching are too profound to their heathen mind to be grasped yet, and they will return to their villages to throw all their influence in the scale against any of their people becoming Christians.

But see! amongst the crowd of listeners is a tall, sharp-featured man. He is not a farmer: you can tell that by his dress. He is not a shopkeeper either, for he has a refined look, as though he got his living by his pen. He is very attentive, and, as he seems to catch the drift of our argument more easily than the stolid-looking men around, we address ourselves particularly to him. He perceives this, and becomes still more attentive. As we reiterate the strong points in our discourse, he waves his head slowly from side to side as though our thoughts were flowing into his brain, and he was endeavouring to assimilate them more rapidly by this physical process. We stop by and by and ask him how he likes what he has heard. He assures us that he is profoundly impressed. "Every word that you have uttered is Heaven's truth," he says, "and men ought to believe. The difficulty is, you know," and here he looks keenly and sharply at us, "the Chinese are bad, and, moreover, they are bound by customs that have been handed down from their remote ancestors; and so it is next to impossible to act in defiance of these, and yet be tolerated by our relatives and neighbours." We find after he has left that he is employed in some official capacity in the mandarin's court up the street, and that he has been sent by his superior to report on the character of the doctrines that are preached by the barbarian. Let us hope that he will give a tolerably true account of what has been said.

This region proved to be a most difficult one to influence. There were two reasons for this. The people generally were comfortably off, and consequently were not disposed to deny themselves the luxuries and the vices that men who have the means indulge in in China. A rich village is always more difficult of access to the preacher than a poor one. The good gifts of God, instead of disposing men to worship Him, have too often the very opposite effect. Another great impediment to the spread of the Gospel was the social condition of this region. The villages were numerous, and some of them contained several thousands of people. As a general rule, the members of each belonged to the same clan, and consequently were more or less related to each other. Ages ago, the founder of the clan came and settled there. His descendants have prospered and multiplied, and they have ramified into various family branches, which in their turn have become numerous and powerful. Questions that affected particular individuals or families only were decided by themselves; but those that touched the whole clan could not thus be settled. Not only the heads of the tribes, but also every individual member of them, with true democratic freedom, felt themselves free to express their opinion either in praise or in condemnation of them. Now there was one particular phase of their religious life in which the whole clan was deeply affected, and that was their ancestral worship. A large building was erected in some prominent place in the village, where the tablets that were supposed to contain the spirits of their forefathers were placed. Annually, with great pomp and ceremony, the clan assembled, and the leading men offered sacrifices to these, and implored the dead from whom they were descended to protect them, and to send them happiness and prosperity. When a man became a Christian he could, of course, take no part in such worship. This was considered monstrous by his fellow clansmen. What! not worship the dead that had given them birth, and had watched over them for generations, and had guided them through the perils of ages, and had made them a strong people to-day. There was no wrong that seemed to them so heinous as this. One of the bitterest terms of reproach that is still constantly hurled against the Christians is that they have renounced their forefathers. This to a heathen Chinaman implies the very depth of wickedness, and shows a depravity of heart that even the vilest in the community would indignantly repudiate.

The knowledge of Christianity has now spread so widely in that region, and has made such a favourable impression upon the people generally, that men do not suffer as they used to do, when they avow their determination to worship God. In those early days it required a great deal of courage, and a good deal of the spirit that led our martyrs to the stake to dare to declare in the face of their clan that henceforward they would no more take a part in the services that were deemed essential to the well-being of the tribes. Was it any wonder that there was the fiercest indignation against them? Their kinsmen had no knowledge of God. They had a dim conception that Heaven in some mysterious way protected men; but this belief was too vague a one, and besides, they had no authoritative revelation on this subject, and so they got no comfort from it. Their dead friends were a reality to them. They were allied to them by the nearest of all ties— that of blood. Who could love them as much as they, and whose heart could be so moved towards them as theirs? The man who gave up this belief was not simply a renegade: he was a traitor to his own kin, and should be shown no mercy. His condition, indeed, was sometimes a most unhappy one. He was despised and hated by his neighbours, and I have known of cases where the man's wife indignantly refused to live with him. He was denied the ordinary protection of the laws; his crops were cut down by night; his potatoes were dug up by unknown hands; his cattle were stolen from him, and, if he appealed to the elders of the village for redress, he was scornfully dismissed with the reply that he had forfeited all his rights by becoming a Christian. In spite of all this, men under the impulse of the new faith, and even gentle, timid women, whose hearts had been melted by the story of the Cross, dared to brave the anger of their relatives and of the clan.

The Gospel had not been long preached in Koan-Khau before several persons professed their faith in Christ. One of these was a young man that kept a cake shop in one of the principal streets of the town. He was naturally a thoughtful and earnest man, and the exalted truths of Christianity had a special attraction for him. The question of religion was to him a most serious one, and now that he had obtained what he believed to be the true one, he was prepared to make any sacrifices that might be demanded of him for it. The time very speedily came when he was to be tested. It is the custom in every town to hold public services in honour of the idols in it, at particular times of the year. Each district appoints a head man, who arranges about the feast and the theatrical performances, and who also collects from the public the sums in which they have been assessed to defray expenses. This man, with a number of his followers, applied to the cake-maker for his amount. He told them that he had become a Christian, and could no longer pay as he had been accustomed to do. They said they had no objection to his worshipping any God he pleased, so long as he conformed to existing usages. He was positive in his refusal, and they went away. Next day they returned and proposed a scheme by which he might be relieved, whilst at the same time they would not lose his subscription. They suggested that he might increase his rent by the amount due, and then the landlord could settle with them. "They did not wish," they said, "to quarrel with him, because hitherto they had been good neighbours together. He was an honest, industrious man, and they liked him, and were anxious to come to some arrangement that would prevent ill-feeling." The Christian sturdily refused to agree to this plan, as it would not be honest for him to do so, seeing that he would still be paying for the support of an idol that he disbelieved in. They again reasoned with him, and appealed to him to give in, on the ground that his case would afford a precedent for others. The head man said: "Suppose that you are allowed exemption: of course other persons in the street may claim the same. And supposing that the whole street should decide to follow your example, then how would the temple service be kept up, and who would pay for the feasts in honour of the idol? The whole thing would then collapse."

The man replied with a smile that this was what he hoped and longed for. "The idols," he said, "were the work of men's hands, and they had been the source of infinite sorrow and mischief to the Chinese. The sooner they were abolished from the country the better it would be for the nation." The head man was struck with the boldness of this Christian in the way he spoke about their gods. He seemed to have no dread of their vengeance, and no fear that they would afflict him in his person, or ruin him in his business. They were amazed, but in no way convinced, so they calmly told him that he must either pay or be prepared for such treatment as he would find would make it impossible for him to do business in that town. Before long he found that this was not an idle threat. During the next few months, he was so harassed by those in authority, and deserted by his customers, that he had to shut up his shop, and remove to Amoy.

Amongst the very first believers, was a man who was destined to hold a prominent place in the church afterwards, and to be the means of the conversion of a large number of his countrymen. Humanly speaking he was about the very last man that one would have dreamt of accepting the truth. Let us describe him. He was a tall, slim man, with a bright piercing eye, and he had a restless, uneasy look about his face, as though he had something on his mind, and was constantly perplexed with the thought as to how he could get rid of it. He was a highly excitable and nervous fellow, and could not sit quietly for two minutes at a time. His hands or his legs were constantly in motion, and on the slightest provocation he would get heated and talk with tremendous energy. Although his face did not betoken any very great strength of character, there was sufficient in the strong lines about his mouth to indicate that he could be very determined if he liked. Just a short time before I met him, he had been one of the very worst characters in his village. He had been a gambler, and a constant companion of men of the lowest description, such as are usually found in the gambling dens in China. He was, moreover, a thief, for his losses at the gambling table had to be made up in some way or other, and the easiest method was by joining a band that used to prowl about at night, and rob and plunder in the villages far and near. It is an extraordinary fact that in spite of the degraded and vicious character of this man, he held a most important sacred office in his village. He was an idol medium. As the idol cannot reveal its own will, or give replies to the worshippers, some one is selected to fulfil these duties. The person who is supposed to be a suitable one is taken to the temple, where certain noisy ceremonies are gone through, whereupon the spirit of the god enters the man, and he is then competent to speak authoritatively in the name of the idol. This service is conducted at night time. The party gathers at the main entrance of the temple, where two or three small oil lamps serve but to reveal the darkness. The grim idol can be dimly seen sitting in its shrine, with its attendant figures by its side. The group of men that are chanting in a steady, monotonous voice the charms that are supposed to bring the spirit, are usually men of no reputation in the village. There is no scholar in his long robe present, and no man of influence stands by to do honour to the idol. The men look fit for scenes of darkness, and remind one of Macbeth's witches making their incantations round their cauldron. On they go for hours in the darkness. The voices at times grow louder and more excited, and the beat on the drum more vigorous. All at once the medium, who has begun to sway his body from side to side as if to invite supernatural influences, begins to be violently affected. He dances and leaps in the air; the beat of the drum becomes more rapid, and the voices of the men louder and shriller. The wildest confusion reigns. It seems as though some horrid scene from the infernal regions were being enacted on earth, and the devils had been let loose for a time to carry on their orgies amongst men. Finally the medium drops down on the ground terribly exhausted, and quivering with excitement. He is now supposed to be qualified to interpret the mind of the god, and to stand between it and its worshippers. It has always been an extraordinary thing to me that the Chinese, who are an exceedingly shrewd and intelligent people, should be content with a system that allows such men to occupy the high position of being at times inspired by their gods, whilst they know that their moral character is exceedingly bad. The man I have above described was a most daring medium, and was not at all restrained by any fear of the idol from giving forth opinions that were never dictated to him by it. He pretended to be inspired by it, but as he has since told me, he was influenced only by his own passions. If his statements or promises were not fulfilled, no blame was attached either to him or to the idol. Any failure was always put down to the want of sincerity on the part of the worshipper, for want of sincerity was always understood to vitiate any request that might be offered to the idol. Passing the church one day, he was so influenced by the truth, that in process of time he gave up his position as a medium, and became an honest and virtuous member of the community. He at once gave up his gambling and his midnight adventures, as well as the company of his loose companions, and began to cultivate the few small fields that his father had left him. After a time, being conspicuous for his earnestness, and the zeal with which he preached the Gospel to his countrymen, he was taken into our training institution, and for many years he has been an energetic and successful preacher of the Gospel.

As the church began to grow in numbers, it was deemed advisable to commence work in some of the large villages and market towns in the district.

These had been for years visited by all kinds of mission agencies. Missionaries had itinerated from village to village; native preachers had expounded Christianity, and shown from their own experience the blessings it brings to men, and Bible colporteurs had sold the word of God in every village and hamlet, and had explained the wonderful revelation it contained of God's love for the world. Besides all these, the Christians in their own homes, and amongst their neighbours, had by a purer life, and by the explanation of the cause of the marvellous transformation that had often taken place in themselves, been doing a work that was in some respects even more effective than that of any of the above. This necessary, preliminary work was often very trying and fatiguing. The great sun was burning overhead, and everything one touched was hot. The effort to keep oneself cool seemed enough to absorb all one's energies. As we entered a village the people would throng around us with looks full of curiosity. They were not as responsive as we, with our strong faith, expected they ought to be. Some were indifferent, others were hostile, whilst some again were simply puzzled with the novelty of men going about as we were to preach such strange doctrines. As we began to speak every voice was hushed, and every face was turned to us; but there was a lack of intelligent understanding of what we said that oppressed us. The simplest truths were explained as though we were talking to children, but they could not grasp them. The *vis inertiæ* of heathenism is a force that paralyzes the spiritual faculties, and renders men incapable at first of comprehending spiritual truths. It is a factor, however, with which we have to deal every time we come in contact with a heathen audience. As we proceeded with the exposition of the very elements of religion we saw a gradual change come over the faces before us. A look of intelligence flashed over them. We took our illustrations from nature around us. The mountains, bathed in the light of the great Eastern sun; the banyan tree, under which we stood, whose leaves were silvered with the rays that came flashing down upon them, and that poured in streams through the boughs and branches upon the faces of the crowd; and the green crops of rice that raised their heads to the sun and drank in the light that was to turn them into golden harvests that would fill the homes of our listeners with gladness—these they could understand. Through them their thoughts were taken up to the great Father, the Creator of them all, and now they became absorbed as they listened. We spoke again of a Saviour that had come to redeem men from sin, and to comfort them in the sorrows and miseries of life. A still brighter flash lighted up their faces. We felt a current of sympathy flow between them and us. We forgot the day was hot. Our fan was poised motionless in our hand, as we caught the signs of the increasing interest. We were all unconscious that the perspiration was streaming down us. We had touched them with the Divine message, and we had the ecstacy of feeling that the hearts around us were as human as our own, and could be reached by the same Gospel that had filled ours with hope and gladness. By and by we left them with friendly greetings, and with urgent requests that we should come and visit them again before long.

And thus the work went on for years. Sometimes amidst clouds, and sometimes amidst sunshine, but always with an unfaltering faith in the Gospel, we taught men about God. The knowledge of Him had died out, and in His place was left the grim, repulsive idol, the only representative of the great loving Father. Men, it is true, talked of Heaven, but that embodied no person, and within it there was no great heart that throbbed in sympathy with men. To get men to understand that there is a God is apparently a very easy matter, and yet it is an exceedingly difficult one, and one that absorbs the energies of the missionary in the early stages of every new work. Some men seem instinctively and at once to grasp the idea, but the masses do not. The conception of a personal God is a tremendous revelation to a pure heathen, and it is long before the picture becomes a living one that influences and comforts his life. The places selected for the new work were generally like Koan-Khau. They were either market towns, or large villages, and were in a smaller degree centres that attracted to them the surrounding population. Our great aim was to economize our strength. By occupying such places we could reach large numbers without the necessity of ourselves visiting every village and hamlet in the district. In this way our influence was far-reaching, and in course of time men and women, who recognised in the Gospel a Divine message to themselves, gathered round us, and small churches were founded that have grown in prosperity, and that are to-day self-supporting. Besides the original church in Koan-Khau, there are now five others scattered throughout this district, that for

A LADY AT HER TOILETTE.

many years have paid their own pastors and preachers, and that carry on their own church work as intelligently as any of the old established churches in England. We believe that the Chinese should support the Christian religion. They support idolatry, and that very liberally. We always make it a special point that every mission church shall become self-supporting at the earliest period possible. The Chinese are to be the evangelizers of China. In educating these native churches to become independent of foreign aid, we are really training them for the mighty work that lies before them in the future.

It was most interesting to watch the elective process by which the Gospel selected out of the crowds that listened in the market places and the churches, not simply those whose hearts were in deepest sympathy with it, but also those who were to become distinguished preachers of it. The history of one of these is an exceedingly beautiful one, and as it is illustrative of this very process, I shall proceed to give it. The person I refer to was a Chinese scholar of the name of Tay. He was originally of a good family, but he had for many years been a most inveterate smoker of opium, and consequently had squandered away his fortune, till now he was a very poor man. At the time my story opens, he was a teacher in the family of a wealthy merchant, near one of our churches, who was as great a smoker as himself. Having heard that the foreigners were preaching certain new doctrines, they determined to go and hear for themselves what they were. On their arrival at the church, the wealthy man stopped at the door. He would not compromise himself further than that.

The scholar advanced boldly into the middle of the room where the Christians were holding their service, and stood looking at the preacher. How little did he then dream that he had come to a great crisis in his life, and that the kingdom of heaven had come nigh to him. Let us look at him for a moment as he stands there. He is a man of medium height, slouchy and disreputable looking, as a consequence of his opium habit. His face has that pallid, death-like look that opium after a time invariably stamps upon it. It is naturally a serious one, and one would never dream that mirth could ever lighten it up; but when a smile does come, it flashes through it like the early sun upon the landscape that has just emerged out of night. The more the face is studied the more irresistibly are we drawn towards it. The mouth is somewhat stern, showing strong will, but the background is a kindly one, and we can see there sympathy, and tenderness, and a heart that could be moved to noble deeds were he delivered from his vice. One thing is certain, he is a scholar. His pallid face, and his shabby looking clothes, and the dissipated air that envelopes him cannot take away the refined, scholastic look that marks the literary man.

The preacher stops for a moment and politely requests him to be seated. He at once takes his seat on the nearest bench, much to the disgust of the merchant, who presently returns home, inveighing as he goes against the stupidity of Tay for thus identifying himself with these Christians. At the conclusion of the service, the preacher got into conversation with him, and expressed his pleasure at seeing him, and hoped he would come again. He assured him that the sole object they had in view in assembling together was to worship the true God, the same that their fathers in ancient times revered. "Of course," he continued, "as a scholar, you are aware that long before the time of Confucius our forefathers worshipped God. The idols of to-day are never once mentioned in the Confucian classics. God is continually spoken of. He is the Creator of the heavens and the earth, and of all things; but I will give you a book in which you can read of His great power." He then handed him the Old Testament, and asked him to read the first chapter in it. The scholar sat down and began to read to himself. He had not read many lines before a look of astonishment came over his face. Turning to the preacher, he asked him who had written these words. It was explained that they were Divinely inspired, and had been given to man by God to describe how the world had been created. The scholar listened with profound attention, and then proceeded with his reading. It was evident when he had finished the chapter that he was most seriously impressed. "I was delighted," he afterwards told me, "with the story of creation. In all my reading in Chinese I had never met with anything that could equal it. There was a dignity and a grandeur about the description that captivated me. I felt it was worthy of the subject." Unconsciously to himself, he had with the reading of that Divine story taken his first step towards God. He was easily persuaded to remain and take dinner with the Christians and stay for the afternoon service. Excepting during the time of public worship the day was spent in conversing about Christianity, and it was late in the evening when he reached the house of his employer. There he was received with jokes and sneers, which, however, soon ended when the serious business of the evening, viz., opium smoking, began. The whole of next Sunday was spent with the Christians. To his great delight he now heard more fully of Christ the Redeemer. He learnt that He had come to save men from their sins, and for this purpose had died to deliver men. He expressed a wish to become His disciple. He was told that he could be one, but he must be prepared to give up his opium. This he readily agreed to, and made the instant determination to do so at once. He was advised not to do this, but to give it up gradually. He was told of the danger there was to his life, after smoking for so many years, and that to renounce the habit by degrees was the safer course. He refused to listen to this advice. He said: "I wish to become a disciple of Jesus; opium smoking is inconsistent with such a profession, therefore I'll never smoke again as long as I live." The strength of the man's character may be inferred from this determination. He knew that he would have to suffer terribly, but he was willing.

When he returned home in the evening, his employer told him to come away and take his opium. "Everything is ready for us," he said. The scholar said: "I have become a Christian, and I am never going to smoke again." The merchant looked incredulously at him, and smiling grimly, said: "You'll change your mind before midnight, and when you do, the opium is there ready for you." Midnight saw him suffering. The opium craving was upon him. Every bone in his body ached, an intolerable lassitude that made life a burden crept over him. Sleep fled from his eyes as completely as though they had never been made to come under its influence. Thoughts ran in quick succession through his brain, as though chased by some demon. A spirit of restlessness came over him, which he could not control. It seemed as though the outside world had lost its power over him, and he was absorbed in a fierce conflict with the forces that made up his own individuality. Relief for all this was close at hand if he chose. In the next room the tray was spread with all the requirements of the opium smoker. A few whiffs of the pipe and the man would be himself again. The fevered brain would rest, the pains and aches that tortured him would cease, and by and by sweet sleep would close his eyes in happy forgetfulness of his sorrows. But not a single step does he take towards the room. The pipe and he have bidden good-bye for ever. There is a new force in his life, even Christ, that holds him true to his purpose. He believes that He can save him, and though it be through fire and suffering he will trust in Him to deliver him. And so the long weary night drags on. The pains increase, the thoughts troop more wildly through his brain, his eyes seem to be on fire, but still no step does he take in the direction of the next room. The same power that kindled the puritan spirit in Englishmen in days gone by was touching this Chinese scholar, and bringing him into the same line with men whose lives have stamped themselves upon history.

Days go on that seem endless, and nights more dreary still that seem eternal, and yet there is no relief. He can do no work; he can settle down to nothing, and as for sleep, ah! that will never come to him again. If he could but get this glare out of his eyes, he thinks he would feel relieved; but though it is midnight and darkness is everywhere, they feel as though the mid-day sun was shining straight upon them. Five or six days pass in this awful struggle, and then the fierce tortures begin to abate. He can sleep at last, and forget himself for a brief season. Each day increases his comfort, until he is finally free, and he now feels he can begin life again with a grander, nobler purpose, than ever he has felt before.

He loses his position as teacher, but he is at once engaged to take charge of one of our Christian schools. After a time he becomes a preacher, and finally he is elected by one of our most influential churches to become its pastor. Many years have elapsed since he passed through this fiery ordeal, but the impressions that it left upon his mind are still strong and vivid. I said to him some time ago, after we had been talking together of those days of trial: "Since you gave up opium, have you ever had the least inclination to go back to it again?" He looked at me steadily for some time, without replying to me, and then a pleasant smile lit up his face, as he said very earnestly, "Never"; and then a shadow chased away the smile, and he became absorbed in thought. I knew he was going over the tragic scenes in his life, and I sat silently by, whilst I thanked God that He had given such a noble man to the Church.

Twenty-eight years have elapsed since the first building was rented in Koan-Khau. Many workers have had the happiness of sharing in the building of the churches in this region. Many a pain and sorrow have they had in their conflict with the forces of heathenism, but their joys have infinitely outnumbered the griefs they have had to endure. To-day the market town is still as crowded as ever, and farmers throng in from the region around, and the great mountains look down upon it; but a change has come over the place since the first missionaries preached in its streets. A thriving church now meets there in a large commodious building, whilst scattered over the plain four others stand out as prominent objects from the idol temples, as places where Christian congregations meet on the Sabbath to worship God.

In addition to these, across the plain and over an arm of the sea, but still in the same county of Tong-an, or Eastern Peace, is the church of Tung-a-be, with its ten mission stations. Five years passed away after the renting of the building in Koan-Khau before serious work began here. At first there seemed insuperable difficulties in the way of the spread of the Gospel. The people were fierce and turbulent. Great clans, that were constantly fighting with each other, held this region, and defied all law. Travellers had to go in companies, and even then had to pay blackmail to avoid being robbed. Pirate boats swarmed from the numerous bays and inlets, and went far afield to plunder, for the fame of these men of Eastern Peace had gone before them, and few cared to fight with them. To-day Tung-a-be is the largest and most active of all the churches in our Mission. Most enthusiastic and laborious are the members in preaching the Gospel to the heathen, as its numerous branch churches can attest. The Gospel has indeed proved to be "the power of God unto salvation" to many a soul in this region, and our faith looks forward to a time in the near distance when our churches shall be largely increased throughout the whole country round.

CHAPTER VI.

THE COUNTY OF HUI-AN; OR, GRACIOUS PEACE.

THE story I have to tell in this chapter opens in the year 1866, in an out-of-the-way village, in the county of Hui-an, or Gracious Peace. The situation of this village is a most picturesque and beautiful one. Just outside of it, Toa-bu, or the "Great Mother" rises abruptly from the plain, and towers up amidst the peaks and mountain-tops that range themselves around it, a conspicuous mark to a large part of the county. In front of it there flows a stream that comes out of the heart of the mountain, its waters pure and sparkling, and as yet undefiled by their touch with the outer world. It never dries up, for its fountains repose deep in the bosom of those everlasting hills; and no summer's drought, nor fiery-faced sun can penetrate to where they lie. Its music, too, never dies out, for jutting rocks, and stones worn smooth, and curves and winding passages, and miniature falls make it sing an endless song.

In this village there lived a farmer and his wife, with their four sons. Their house was a large, capacious one, and evidently had been built in the days when the farmer's ancestors were in a prosperous condition. Times had changed, however, and grim, gaunt poverty stalked about the home. This was not owing to the bad management of the wife. She was a woman with much force of character. She had shrewd common sense, and it was due to her superior wisdom, and to her heroic endurance, that the family was able to keep up an appearance, that was not sustained by any resources they had at their command. The miserable condition of the home was entirely the result of the misconduct of the husband. He was a wretched little creature, and entirely wanting in those moral qualities that enable a man to perform the duties of life with even a minimum amount of success. His want of moral stamina was seen in the vices into which he had fallen. He was an opium smoker, and in addition to that, a confirmed gambler. He was a constant visitor to the neighbouring market-town, where the gambling houses and the opium dens drew to themselves the dissipated and the abandoned from all the villages round about. This life soon told upon his home. The farm was neglected. One after another of his ancestral fields was sold to pay his gambling debts, and to provide him with opium. The crops in front of the house still waved beautiful and green, watered by the mountain stream, but they brought no sense of relief to the suffering wife and her hungry children, for they belonged to another; and when the time of harvest came, they would not be gathered into their empty barns. Things went on from bad to worse, till it became a serious question whether it would not be necessary to sell some of the children to provide the rest with food. The mother resisted this. She knew that in the end this would result in the entire breaking up and dispersion of the family. The children would be sold one by one, and then she would follow, and finally the ancestral home would pass into other hands. The gambling-houses and the opium dens have no conscience, and no remorse; they are omnivorous in their appetite. They care not for family ties, or mother's tears, or whether hearts are broken or not. They are reckless of human sorrow.

Just at this crisis, when the hour seemed the very darkest, and starvation had come up to the very doors, it was agreed that the husband should travel south to Amoy, and see whether he could not find employment there, and somehow or other retrieve his fortunes. Imagine the gambler and the opium smoker, ruined and beggared, starting to make his fortune, with two vices dogging his steps, that would spoil any human fortune that might come to him. Before he begins his journey, let us stop for a moment to consider this family. I presume that if we were to travel through the whole county, and examine every family in it, there would be very few in it that would give less promise of becoming a spiritual power to this region than it. The husband was a reckless gambler, that would sit night after night amongst desperate characters, and madly risk the money that would have fed his children. The mother was sad and worn with anxiety, and the little ones pale and hungry. What moral power could ever come from this home? We should answer, none. And yet God had decided that Christianity was to be given to this county by it, and that the first message that was to result in the building of churches, and the gathering in of men and women, who were to make a noble profession of faith in Him, was to be uttered by the lips of this degraded opium smoker.

The man started for Amoy. He smoked his opium before he set out, though his family was almost starving around him, for he could take no journey till he had done that. He left sorrowful hearts behind him, for his wife was too sensible not to know that, with his habits, failure was a certainty. On arriving at Amoy, he could get no employment. He was a little, insignificant-looking man, with the brand of opium stamped upon his face, and so men were shy of engaging him to do work for them. He consequently before long drifted to a small market town, named "Sea Village," where some people from his own district lived. He hoped through them to be introduced to some method by which he could gain his living; but he wished especially to borrow some money from them, for the terrible opium craving that came upon him daily was a demon that tortured him with infinite pain, and his resources were nearly all exhausted. Fortunately, there was a small church in this village, and having nothing to do, he one day sauntered in. Let us pause here to mark the wonderful way in which God has thus far been leading him. Step by step he has travelled from his far-off home in the north, till he has reached this out-of-the-way village, and now he has come to the very house where he is to learn how his fortunes are to be retrieved, and his home to be made glad with prosperity, and how the fields that are green with luxuriant rice shall come back again to him, and how the ancestral home need never be sold to strangers, whilst he is alive at least. The possibility of all this lies within his very grasp, as he enters the church, not far from the water-side.

The Gospel seemed to have an especial attraction

for this man, and he listened to it with perfect delight. Never before had he heard truths that touched his heart, as those, that the preacher expounded, did. Before long he became a true convert to Christianity, and as a proof of this, he began the painful process of curing himself of opium. What that means, only an opium smoker can tell. After severe suffering he found himself free, and then, for the first time in his life, he was a real man. The Gospel had given him the nerve to do what the entreaties of his wife, and the wan and haggard faces of his children, and the dread of ruin had been unable to effect. In the course of time he was baptized, and then there came to him that profound spiritual experience that every truly converted man or woman invariably passes through. He had a great longing to preach this Gospel, that had saved him, to his fellow-men. He came to Mr. Stronach, and told him of his anxiety to return home to let his wife and children see the change that had been wrought in him. His chief desire, however, was to tell them of Christ, the Saviour of the world, and to let the people of his own village, and the men of Gracious Peace, hear the good news that had gladdened his own heart. Mr. Stronach listened with delight, and at once gave him authority to arrange for renting a house in his village, where Christian services could be held, and promised to come and preach himself as soon as it would be wise for him to do so.

He starts out for his home, a man over whom a marvellous change has passed. He is not a hero, for he is lacking in those moral qualities that constitute such; and, moreover, the scars of his old vices are still visible in him. He is a man, however, that God has chosen to do such a work as many a greater man might have gone down on his knees and besought God to let him have the honour of doing. He travels along the same great road by which he came, but he is no longer oppressed by a vice that was eating out his very life. He mingles amongst the crowds that travel with him, but the low passions that filled his soul have fled, and he talks to them of a Gospel that has delivered him, and can equally save all other men. He is a fearless preacher. He has a pleasant smile, and a ready knack of avoiding unpleasant ways of presenting the truth, that makes even those that disagree with him willing to listen to him. He has an inimitable manner of assuming, as a matter of course, that what he preaches is the truth, which half overcomes an opponent. There is no hesitating, and no eagerness to defend his position, as though he thought it were assailable. He will take any amount of pains in explaining it; but defend it, never, for it is the eternal truth of God, and needs no defence. As well try and justify the sun when it is filling the landscape with beauty, or the crops that have just turned into a golden colour, and give the promise of plenty to those whose lives depend upon them.

The preaching of the Gospel in the little village, under the shadow of the great mountain, produced great excitement far and wide throughout the county. Men came from every direction to find out what these new doctrines that were being preached meant; the result being, that the Sunday services were attended by some that were destined in the future to become preachers themselves, and founders of Christian work in their own villages. Ere long this new religion was widely talked about, in market towns, where men gathered to buy and sell, and in villages on the mountain side men discussed it. They were all unconscious, during these discussions, that new forces had already entered their county that were to set men thinking; and instead of the eternal monotony of the common-place thought supplied by idolatry, their minds were to be exercised by ideas which in time would completely change the character of society. The congregation increased in size, and, singular to say, the serious part of it was mainly composed of people from other parts. In the course of a year, Mr. Stronach visited the place, and, after a careful examination of the candidates for baptism, selected twenty, whom he baptized, and who thus constituted the first Christian Church in the county of Gracious Peace. This took place on the seventeenth of March, 1867, a memorable day in the history of the church. The success thus far was remarkable. A year ago the very name of Christianity was unknown; and this out-of-the-way village, sunk in idolatry, gave no promise that the message of life would first be given to the county by it, and that, too, by the mouth of one of its most depraved citizens. After the lapse of so short a period, about forty persons regularly met for the worship of God, twenty of whom were members of the new church.

It must not be supposed that all this was accomplished without opposition. Just in proportion to the hold that Christianity took upon the people, was the active hatred of the more bigoted of the heathen aroused. This, in the very nature of things, must always be the case. An eternal antagonism, as was predicted by Christ, must ever exist between it and the world. A Christian, by his very faith, is prevented from taking a neutral position; in fact, he has to assume an offensive one. This was the case with these early converts. The idols had at once to be renounced, and either broken up or burned. The ancestral tablets, around which gathered so many hallowed associations, and which were the visible ties that bound them to their departed fathers and mothers, had to be destroyed, or buried on the hillside, where none else should know the secret, for around them centred the most profound worship that the Chinese offer to anything. Many local customs and feasts, inextricably bound up with their social life, had to be given up. All this excited the hatred of their relatives, or the more ardent of the idolaters, who were jealous of the honour of their gods, for they were wise enough to perceive that there was a power in this religion, were it allowed to spread, that would completely overthrow the old faiths that had come down to them from their fathers. The most potent enemies of the Gospel, however, are usually the scholars in the villages, because of the influence they wield over the uneducated. They cannot tolerate any teaching except that of Confucius, and so they rouse the passions of their followers by their contemptuous pictures of the foreigner, and their appeal to their patriotism to maintain the honour of the famous men who for so many ages have been the teachers of China. Fortunately, the influence of the scholars in this village under the great mountain was neutralized by some of the leading men in it becoming Christians.

One of the head men, aged seventy-five, was one of the most earnest of the band that was baptized. There was, unquestionably, a special providence in the selection, not only of the man who was to commence the work, but also of the place. Hidden away, almost under the shadow of the "Great Mother," and far removed from the great centres where the opposition might have been fierce, it was just the locality for the Gospel to get a quiet footing, from whence it could ultimately spread to every part of the county.

The preaching of the Gospel was, in the mean time, vigorously carried on in the surrounding villages, and excursions were made to the more distant ones, where some of the Christians resided. In this way the truth spread, and converts were gradually added to the church. In course of time the church was moved from the village to a small market town, on the great road, about a mile away, named Iah-poa. The population was larger, and the numbers that daily passed by the doors of the new building were very great. For a long time after the removal, the church was in a very unsatisfactory condition. It seemed to make no impression on the place, for the members became listless, and wanting in that enthusiasm without which Christianity fails to be a power over the heathen.

During the last two or three years, a remarkable change has come over the church, due almost entirely to the influence of two men who used to have about the worst reputation of anybody in all the neighbourhood. One of these I shall describe, as I saw him on my first visit after he had been converted. He was a little humpbacked man, of insignificant appearance, but with a shrewd, common-sense looking face. It was worn, and somewhat haggard, as though he had passed through a deal of suffering; but there was a quiet look of satisfaction in it, indicating a happy state of mind. He was a citizen of Iah-poa, and had for years kept a gambling-house in it. It was the resort of all the gamblers for miles round, and it had witnessed many a scene of wickedness and dissipation. A few months previously he had gone out of his mind, and had wandered wildly about the country. The temples seemed to have a special attraction for him, but he got no relief from any of them. His relatives made many vows to the idols, and presented offering after offering to them, but all in vain. One day he happened to go into the church, when the preacher spoke to him of Jesus, and His power to cast out evil spirits. The story he heard soothed him. He gradually quieted down. He came again and again, and in a few days his reason came back to him. His marvellous recovery made a great impression upon the villagers, some of whom became regular attendants at the services. His own heart was filled with intense gratitude to God, and he seemed to take a great delight in telling others of the wonderful cure He had effected for him. I watched the play of his features as he told it. His face darkened as he spoke of his former life, and his gambling experiences; then a look full of sadness succeeded, as he described his mental sufferings, and his hopeless despair; and then his face was suffused with a smile of happiness, as he spoke of the return of his reason, and the deliverance that Christ had given him from his old life of sin.

As I looked at the scene before me, I could hardly

believe that it was a real one. A group was gathered round the man, absorbed in the story he was telling, whilst his son, a tall, strapping young fellow stood by, bending tenderly and lovingly over his father. Is this man who speaks so pathetically, and so devotedly, the quondam gambler, that has been the cause of the ruin of so many? How soon he has forgotten the language of the gaming-table, and learnt that of the Christian. The story he tells cannot be true. It must be one of those tales that the story-tellers rehearse with such dramatic power and vividness in the hearing of the street crowds, but which lie within the region of romance, and are an impossibility in actual life. It is no fiction, thank God. The figures before me are all real. The men that stand listening have come out of heathenism, and some of them could tell a story almost as strange as his own. The man himself, not long ago, was a wild maniac, a terror to his friends, and a misery to himself. His madness is gone, and so, too, have the dice and the cards, and the gathering of bad men, and the scenes of dissipation. See him as he talks! what a power he exerts over men that a few months before would have shrunk with perfect horror from him. As he goes over the tragedy of his life he touches every heart with pity, and then again faces are lighted up, and eyes glisten as he speaks of the sunshine that has come into his life since he has experienced the comfort of Christ's love. One of the greatest encouragements in missionary work is the belief that the heroic element lies not very far from the surface in every human being, and needs but the touch of a Divine hand to turn the life into poetry and romance.

Were it not for this, we should often turn in hopeless despair from many that we meet in heathen life; whereas in looking over the history of the churches in the Amoy district, I can think of some of the most flourishing of them to-day, that were founded by men whose lives had been notoriously bad and vicious.

The other man, whose story is connected with the spiritual growth of this church, was a very different character from the one I have been describing. He was possessed of considerable force of intellect, and had abilities that gave him great influence over his fellow-men. Some three or four years ago, I was travelling amongst the mountains, and coming to the foot of them, I passed through the hamlet where he lived. At that time he was well known throughout the district as a man thoroughly destitute of principle, and one who for many years had lived by his wits. For thirty-four years he had been an opium smoker, and during that time had dissipated his father's property, till but little of the old man's inheritance was left. He had a great dislike to Christianity, and he used to mock and jeer at the Christians, and write lampoons about them, and paste them on the door-posts of his house for the amusement of the passers-by. Catching sight of me as I passed by his door, his indignation was aroused. "What does this barbarian mean," he said to himself, "by coming into this region, and disseminating his corrupt and pernicious doctrines? The only reason is because he has not yet met with any one that has the ability to meet and overcome him in argument. He has had to deal with farmers and labouring men, and artisans whose minds have never been trained to the discussion of profound questions. Now I feel that I am a better man than he is, so I shall follow him and overthrow him in argument, and make him so ashamed that he will never dare to show his face again in this quarter." Accordingly he followed me along the narrow path that wound by the river side and through the valley where rice crops were growing in the shadow of the mountains, and along the great high road up to the door of the church. Just as I had entered I happened to look round and saw him. I thought: Oh, dear me! what does this man want? I shall have nothing to do with him, for I cannot possibly do him any good. His face was about as bad a one as ever I have seen in China. If ever there was a countenance upon which villain was written, it was his. It was steeped in opium. His clothes were greasy, and shabby looking in the extreme. His eyes were bright and restless, and he had the appearance of one who was perpetually planning profound schemes of wickedness.

I retired to my private room determined not to talk with him, but I could not get him out of my thoughts. My mind became uneasy, and silent questionings prevented me from thinking of any other subject. "This man has evidently come to see me," I said. "Is it fair to remain here whilst he is outside there waiting for me? My commission is to preach to all men, whatever their characters may be; and who am I to decide who is the proper subject for the kingdom?" I at once came out, and found him seated on a bench. He rose and received me with profuse etiquette, for though a scamp he was a gentleman; whilst I, in my best Chinese, politely requested him to be seated. Before commencing to talk with him about religion, I thought it advisable to touch his heart in some way, so that he might have a friendly feeling towards me before we began our discussion. I brought out some foreign biscuits that I had with me, and asked him if he had ever seen such. No, he had not. "Would he like to take a few home with him?" I said, and I placed some in his hands. His grim, bad-looking-face instantly relaxed, and a half smile, like a sudden flash of light upon a thunder-cloud, passed over it, as he bowed his thanks to me.

I then asked him if he had a father. If there is one thing that a Chinaman gets enthusiastic about it is his parents. If he has any heart left, this is a subject that will be sure to touch it. "Oh yes," he replied with enthusiasm, "and would you believe it? he is eighty-seven years old." "Ah! fortunate man," I said, "what a good man you ought to be, since Heaven has been so kind as to spare him so long to you." "Yes," he said. And then he went on to tell of all his father's virtues; and as he dwelt upon these, he became eloquent, and the bad look in his face disappeared, and the repulsive features became sublimed, and for the moment the vicious reprobate had vanished, and I saw before me a man moved by the purest and tenderest feelings. I was amazed. I felt my heart drawn out towards him. I forgot the repulsive feelings I first had. He had proved to me, that in spite of his shabby clothes, and repulsive features, and the impalpable air of dissipation that hung around him, he was still human.

THE COUNTY OF HUI-AN.   141

When he had finished, I said: "Won't you take some biscuits to your father?" and I placed several on the bench in front of him. "He has never seen any, and they will be a novelty and a curiosity to him." The man's eyes sparkled as he received them with many thanks. His heart was touched I could see. And now he was ready for the impartial hearing of a Gospel that up to this time had come to him only through the distorted rumours that had been carried to him by men that understood it as little as himself. For more than an hour we discussed some of the great doctrines of Christianity. He listened with profound attention, and questions were put in a kindly way, as though he were really anxious for information. His demeanour was that of a man who was anxious to know the truth; and never once did it occur to me that he had come that day with the purpose of making me ashamed. At last he said: "Now, sir, I should like to be a Christian, but there is one thing that I can never give up." As he said this the war look flashed into his eyes, and placing his head on one side, he straightened himself up, as though he were trying to shake off the influence I had gained over him. "What is it that you can never give up?" I anxiously inquired. He said: "I can never give up my ancestral worship." This ancestral worship is the profoundest form of faith that the Chinese have. It is the very last thing that a Chinaman gives up when he becomes a Christian. Though intensely idolatrous, there is something very touching about it. The father dies, and at the anniversary of his death the son comes to his tomb and places his offering before it, and he believes that somehow or other the food and the paper money will reach the spirit in the other world, and make it more happy. He never expects to see his father again, but he would fain hope that though gone from him here, the tie is not utterly broken, and that he can still minister to the wants of him he loved so much whilst on earth. I saw by the stern look in his face that we were on dangerous ground, and that were I to declare that ancestral worship must be instantly abandoned, I should lose the man entirely, and convert him into an enemy instead of a friend. I accordingly said to him: "Well then, don't give up your worship, go on with it. The first thing you have to do is to give up your opium. Every other question must be left in abeyance until this, the supreme one in your life, has been settled." As I said these words, a marvellous change came over the man. The defiant look that shone in his eyes and held the pale opium-dyed face in its grasp, gradually died away. The head assumed its natural position, and the body subsided from its stiff, erect attitude, and became limp, just as though some vital force had suddenly been snatched out of it. "I will give up the opium," he said, in a low tone, as though he were measuring the amount of suffering he would have to go through. "I will begin at once, and gradually diminish the quantity until I am finally free from it." Poor fellow! I pitied him, for I knew somewhat of the awful struggle that lay before him. For thirty-four years the opium had been a necessity of his life. During all that time he had never had a single day's release from it. It was the dark shadow that had never left him. Will he be able to give it up? Humanly speaking, never; for there is no human power that can stand face to face with it, and overcome it. It is a demon without remorse and without pity. Human tears don't move it, for it has never wept itself; and ruined homes and broken hearts don't touch it. It twines and coils itself about the life, and though it is crushing it out, and knows that it must perish with its victim, it laughs and shrieks with joy at its own death because it has killed another man.

The last time I saw him, I asked him what it was in my conversation with him that day that had touched his heart, and made him finally determined to become a Christian. "Why," he said, "it was those words of yours, 'go on with your worship, but you must give up your opium.' My heart was deeply moved by them. No man had ever shown himself so interested in my welfare as you had done. Others had scorned me, and looked down upon me, because of my character, but you showed that you cared for me. You allowed me to continue my worship, but you pleaded with me to give up my opium, and be a good son, that I might yet be a comfort to my old father. I knew from that moment that you loved me, and I felt that I could do anything in the world you asked me."

Some months after this, I returned to pay a visit to the church. I found the Christians in great joy about my opium friend. They told me he had been a most regular attendant at the services, and most energetic in his endeavours to get others to become Christians. Whilst we were talking, he came up smiling to me, and I asked him about the opium. "I have given up a half," he said, "and I am gradually lessening the quantity I take daily, so that I am hopeful in time I shall not require to smoke it." I was disappointed. He ought to have been further on the way to freedom; so I said: "Kai, you will never give up opium as long as you live if you remain in this neighbourhood. The opium dens are near you, and your old comrades are about you to tempt you. You must come with me to the missionary hospital, and stay in it till you are thoroughly cured. I see no other way to save you, for the forces around you are too strong for you, and I must take you out of them. Will you go?" "Oh yes," he replied. "I'll do anything you want me, and go wherever you like."

On my return to Amoy, Kai accompanied me to the large city of Chin-Chew, where Dr. Grant had a hospital. When we came to his door, I asked him to remain in the street until I had seen the doctor. This gentleman somewhat demurred to taking in an opium smoker, because he had not much faith in being able permanently to cure such, but after my representing to him that my friend wished to become a Christian, he said: "Well, bring him in, and let me see what kind of a man he is." We were standing in an open courtyard under the spreading branches of a tree, and when Kai appeared the doctor was startled. Gazing at him intently, he said to me in a quick, hurried manner: "This man is a bad man. Send him away from here at once. Just look at his face, what a villainous looking one it is! You ought to be a sufficient judge of character to know that you can do nothing with such a man as that."

The poor fellow stood by fortunately not knowing

SEDAN BEARERS.

anything of what was being said. He was a sad, pathetic picture to look upon. As he stood there with the dark wall as a background, he looked about as dissipated a figure as a painter has ever drawn, and yet he was immensely improved as compared with what he was months before when I first saw him. His clothes were now respectable-looking, and the indescribably evil something that lay behind those bad-looking features, like shadows that darken the hollows of the mountain, had become less marked, whilst through the opium hue on his face there appeared the faintest possible suspicion of the tinge of a colour that was still far off in the distance. I begged the doctor to let him stay, because he was my friend, and because I had faith that he would turn out to be a good man. I knew, besides, that if there was any man in China that could save him it was Dr. Grant. The system that he had established in his hospital was one of the most perfect I have ever seen. It was not simply that he was an exceedingly able medical man. He had the genius of bringing Christianity to bear on his patients in such a loving, forcible way that the hospital had become a powerful centre, from which the truth had gone out to many counties, and many had been the souls that could trace the beginning of their new life to the time when they were being treated in it. I myself have had the privilege of baptizing a goodly number in Gracious Peace who were converted in his hospital. "I wish your friend were better looking," he replied to my urgent request, as he gazed doubtingly and hesitatingly upon him. "If it were not for your recommendation, I should refuse to have anything to do with him. Let him remain, however, and I'll do my best to cure him, though from his looks I have not much faith in him."

In about a month Kai had left the hospital cured, and a better Christian than when he entered it. He went away, too, with the highest admiration on the part of Dr. Grant towards him. The other day I saw the doctor in London, and talking of the time when I brought the wretched opium smoker to be cured, and the terribly dissipated look he had, he said : " If there is one man in China that I have faith in, it is Kai." After his return home he became a great preacher. He travelled amongst the mountains near his home, and the villages in the valleys, and searched out his old opium-smoking comrades, and told them of the Divine love that had saved him. The fame of his conversion filled the whole district. The heathen were amazed, for there was no power in all China that could have wrought such a mighty miracle as this. Even his own family were startled, and could hardly believe in the reality of his conversion. Passing by his home one day, I spoke to one of his sons, and urged him to follow in the footsteps of his father, and become a Christian.

"I cannot do so yet," he said, in a low tone, "for I must wait and see how my father turns out."

He was evidently doubtful about the change, and no wonder that he should be. From the time that he was a child, and through his boyhood, and up into the years of his manhood, he never had had any other picture of his father than that terrible life that had brought misery and poverty upon the home. Time has proved, however, that the change was a real one. The bad, wild look has disappeared. The pale, hollow cheeks have become rounded, and when I last saw him they were slightly tinged with colour ;

but more powerful evidence than all this lies in the awakened church, and the numbers that I see crowd to the services on the Sabbath, who first heard the Gospel from his lips.

The man is himself a standing miracle to me, and yet I never think of him without a dread feeling of anxiety that I cannot control. Is he really for ever free from that awful opium? For thirty-four years it held him in its grip. It controlled his life, and destroyed his manhood, and absorbed his will so completely that he had no thought of resisting it. Has it, indeed, given up its mastery over him? It would seem so, and yet some of its roots may still be imbedded far down in his nature, and some day, in a moment of weakness or temptation, these may again assert their power, and he may once more fall under the awful and mysterious fascination with which opium charms its victims. My hope that this may not happen, is entirely in the grace of God. No power of will, no selfish thought of life, no human affections will save him. Nothing short of Divine power can keep him a free man.

The last time I visited that church sixteen men and women stood up before the Christians and the heathen that crowded the doors and filled up every available standing ground, and told the story of what Christ had done for them. Most pathetic, and most touching were some of them. Opium smokers related how they had found deliverance, and gamblers told how the cards and dice had lost their fascination for them after they had heard the Gospel. Men spoke of the bondage they had been in for years, and how the fear of death had troubled them, and how they had worshipped the idols, but no peace had come to them; but now their hearts were at rest, for Christ had shed His precious blood for them, and had become their Saviour and Redeemer. One woman that had been a sorrow to her husband for years, stood before me with modest look and downcast eyes. I could hardly recognise in her the fierce spirit that had twice compelled her husband to fly from his home to escape her wrath, because he would not worship the idols with her. She confessed how wrong she had been, and how ashamed she felt when she thought of the past. "But I am happy now," she said, "for I have found Christ to be all that my heart can desire, and nevermore shall I wish to worship the idols again."

It is a remarkable thing that these people quickly learn to develop their Christian life very much in the same manner as is done in our home churches. They elect their pastors and deacons, and carry out their church forms as naturally as though they had never been heathen, but had been brought up in Christianity all their lives. Of course they have their own way of doing things, and occasionally I have been highly amused at the methods they pursue.

I remember on one occasion, in one of the churches in this county, it was arranged that there should be an election of deacons. It was in an out-of-the-way country place, where the people were very rustic. Three men were to be appointed, and it was laughable to see how this very simple matter seemed to be one of immense difficulty to the majority of those who had a right to vote. To the bucolic mind it seemed a prodigious undertaking to specify three persons whom they believed capable of exercising the duties of a deacon. The first person that was called upon to come up to the desk and record the names he had selected, seemed quite taken aback. He stood up with a bewildered air, and protested that he did not know whom to choose, in fact he was not aware that there was any one in the church that was fitted for the office. After a little gentle pressure he began to move slowly towards where I was standing, but a kindly bench stood in the way, at which he took his stand, and scratching his head, he declared it was no use his proceeding further, as he did not know how to choose. Various encouraging utterances from the brethren brought him up to where I was waiting for him, but his difficulty seemed only to have increased when he had got there. He looked long and earnestly over the congregation, as though every man in it was a stranger to him, whilst in reality he was familiar with the life and history of every one before him. After a tremendous effort he got out *one* name, and then made a long pause. Being reminded that he had to give two more, he seemed startled, and said: " What! two more!" and then shading his eyes with his left hand he peered long and anxiously at the members, who took the whole thing seriously, and saw nothing funny in it. Then two more names were blurted out, and he went back to his seat with a look of relief on his face. One man, the father of a family, and a sharp, shrewd man in worldly matters, carried on this farce so long that I took him at his word, and made him sit down before he had voted. He was amazed. He could see nothing incongruous in his conduct; in fact it was the proper thing to do.

After the three men had been duly elected, they were called up to be regularly installed. One of them, true to Chinese nature, at once got up, and begged leave to decline the office of deacon. He was not a good walker, he said, and therefore he did not feel competent to fill it. Just imagine a deacon of one of our fashionable English churches declining the office on the ground that he was not a good walker! One of the brethren, who was noted for his humour, suggested that he should buy a horse. He might as well have told him to purchase an elephant or a locomotive, for the man was very poor. The idea, moreover, of a deacon buying a horse to enable him to visit the members of his church was so ridiculous that everybody was amused. A broad grin expanded the faces of every one present, and the black, almond-shaped eyes gleamed and twinkled with suppressed fun. This argument of ridicule was such a powerful one, that the poor man instantly collapsed, and he slowly sidled down into his seat, with a sickly smile on his face, muttering inaudibly to himself.

This mock modesty that I have been describing is a prominent factor in the usages of polite society. Chinese etiquette requires a man to depreciate himself, and to speak of himself in the most derogatory terms, whilst at the same time he may have the most overweening estimate of his own abilities. It was satisfactory to know that these shrewd Chinese, in the midst of all the little farce they had been playing, had all the time been picking out the very persons they ought to have chosen. The three men selected were the very best that could have been elected.

CHAPTER VII.

THE COUNTY OF GRACIOUS PEACE (continued).

Two years have passed by since the Gospel was first preached in the county, and the "Great Mother" from her solemn height looks down upon the growing church that week by week meets for worship in the village at its foot. In addition to the music of the brook, the village is getting accustomed to the sound of tunes that are sung in the churches in far-off England, and which are destined to take a firmer hold upon the people of this county than any of their own secular airs, though transmitted to them through the long course of ages. It is now felt by the Christians that it is time for the Gospel to go forth from the sheltered valley, and occupy a position in some of the great centres, where it could influence greater numbers than here beside this mountain stream, or under the shadow of these great hills. The emblems that Christ used about the Gospel are profoundly true. It is like the mustard seed, and it is like the leaven. It cannot remain stationary. There are forces within it that compel it to spread, and so the valley that will do for its birthplace will be too small for its manhood. There are multitudes in the cities and on the great highways whose hearts have to be touched, and there are men of power, and of thought, and of influence there, who are needed as leaders and workers in this crisis of the county's history.

About five miles distant was the county town. It was not a large place, for it contained only between twenty and thirty thousand inhabitants. It had a

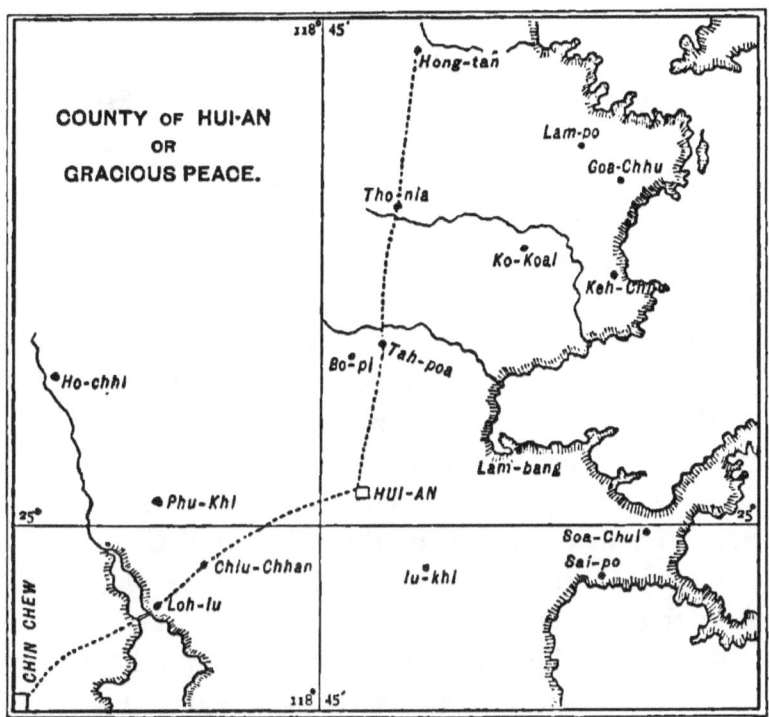

mean and poor appearance, and well corresponded with the general poverty of the county, yet it was a city of great influence. The chief mandarins resided there, as well as a number of prominent scholars who got their living in connection with the law courts. It was, moreover, a great centre of business. Everything that the county could boast was to be purchased there. The fish that was brought in by the great fishing smacks to the famous seaport of "Valiant Warrior" last evening were exposed for sale in its streets next morning by daylight. The men that carried them on their shoulders during the darkness of the night have had a hard time of it. The road, which is seventeen miles long, lies over as heart-breaking a bit of country as it is the lot of poor travellers to pass, as I know by many a painful experience. They have had to travel over hills, and stony paths, and along dry water-courses, where the feet continually sank in sand, till at length jaded and worn they have gained the city in the grey dawn of the morning. Every conceivable article required by the needs or luxuries of the people found its way into the city. No sooner were the gates thrown open at daybreak, at the sound of the morning gun, than crowds of men and women, with eggs, and fowls, and sweet potatoes, and garden produce, and delicious oranges from the next county of the "Pleasure Ground of the Fairies," poured in to dispose of their goods in the public market-places.

When the Christians attempted to rent a house in this place they found themselves opposed by insuperable difficulties. The scholars of the town declared they would allow no foreigner to reside in it to preach his corrupt doctrines, and terrible penalties were threatened against any one that dared to let his house to him. The more fanatical of the heathen, the priests, and those interested in the continuance of idolatry, threw in their influence with the scholars, so that no house could be got throughout the length and breadth of the city. At length, after considerable difficulty, one was obtained in a narrow, dirty street about half a mile away from the town,—a place so obscure that the opponents of Christianity no doubt thought it beneath their notice to make any bother about it. The Christians were exceedingly delighted at the position they had gained, even though in such an unpromising neighbourhood.

And now the work was vigorously carried on from this new centre. The scholars might prevent the Christians from getting a house in the city, but they could not forbid them preaching in it. Accordingly in the busy market places, in the main streets, in the narrow lanes, and even on the steps of the temples, right in front of the idols, the Gospel was proclaimed to the masses. It was also preached in the countless villages that dotted the plains, or nestled in the valleys at the foot of the mountains, on the north, right away to the sea that bounded one side of the county on the east. The result of all this widespread preaching was that in time there grew up a better comprehension of what Christianity was, and a desire in many to believe in it. The people of this county are generally very poor. Their mountains are rugged and barren, and their soil is thin and poor, so that it requires constant and unremitting labour to get even the necessaries of life out of it. The consequence is, that for the great majority of the people life is a continual struggle. The wolf is never very far at any time from their doors, and the dread of impending sorrow must be a perpetual shadow upon their lives. Now the Gospel is full of promise and comfort to such, and the revelation of God as a Father brought men hopes, such as they never knew in their heathen life. The wondrous story of the Cross, too, touched men's hearts, and so they gathered in the narrow street outside the city, and in distant villages, where it was found necessary to open new places of worship; and under the inspiration of the new faith, men that all their lives had worshipped only the idols became fervent preachers of the new Gospel.

The history of one of those that became a Christian at this time is a very interesting one, and illustrates the spiritual experience of a heathen in his passage from darkness into light. The man I refer to was between twenty and thirty years of age, and a person of great vigour of character. Even his very speech showed this, for he always spoke in a sharp, incisive way, as though every word he uttered came from the very depths of his soul. His face was seldom at rest, and his eyes shone and twinkled under the inspiration of hidden thoughts. He was a man, too, prompt in action, and he had a physique that enabled him to endure a great deal of hard labour. He was just the kind of man the church needed in its early pioneer work. One day he happened to go into the city, where he met a Christian who spoke to him about God, and the folly of idolatry. This man gave him instances from their every-day life of how useless the idols were in protecting and comforting men. He went home profoundly impressed. One great thought remained rooted in his mind, namely, that the idols were powerless to save men. To one who has been brought up in Christian lands this is a self-evident truth, and requires merely to be stated to be accepted, but it was not so here. It was a revelation to him. Never had such an idea dawned upon his mind before, and he was perplexed as he thought over it. For three months or so his mind was ill at ease. The truth that the Christian had revealed to him was one that he could not dismiss from his mind, and yet he could not bring himself to accept it. He had always been an intense and earnest worshipper of the idols. More than thirty of them were placed in various parts of his home, that were honoured and worshipped at regular seasons. They were all that his soul had trusted in for years, and he could not consent to abandon them at the bidding of a stranger. Still the power of truth that was working in him was mighty, and he was compelled to listen to it in spite of himself. At the end of the three months a great sorrow fell upon him. Disease attacked his domestic animals. He made earnest appeals to his thirty gods, but still the epidemic did not cease. Then his younger brother died of small-pox, and at the same time heavy rains fell, and the mountain streams came roaring down from the hills, breaking down the embankments of some of his fields, and covering them with sand, so that they became useless. To crown all, one day part of their house, weakened by the long-continued rains, fell down and nearly killed his father. The words of the Christian now came home with intensified force to him. The idols certainly had been proved useless to him in his time of need. He would give up the worship of them. Before he did so, however, he determined to make sure that the Christian religion was all that it was represented to be. His faith was almost shattered, but he would hold on to it until he had proved that Christianity was better than it. He decided to visit Amoy, some seventy-five miles distant, and examine it at its fountain head. It had been first preached there, and the men that came from the far west to promulgate it amongst the Chinese resided there. Amoy was to him what Mecca is to the Mahommedan, or Rome to the Roman Catholic. On his arrival there, he lived at an inn, as he knew no one in the place. The next day he spent in visiting the churches, and in listening to the preaching that was daily carried on in them. He found that they all taught precisely the same doctrines that he had heard in his far-off home. In one of them an old man got up to speak. He was so nearly blind that he could but just see his audience. He had been a Christian for many years, and his eyes, naturally weak, were now failing him. He was not an educated man, or one that was specially gifted in speaking. The power that made his life eloquent was his profound faith in Christ. He had not spoken long before our friend was arrested by his arguments, for they dealt with the very points upon which he was longing for enlightenment. He told how unhappy he had been when he was a worshipper of the idols, how his faith in them had been rewarded by disappointment and sorrow, and how Christ had brought light into his life, and His cross had taken away the burden of sin that used to lie so heavily on his soul. It was not so much the force of argument as the narrative of a soul's experience that touched him into an earnest belief, and loosened the last lingering hold that his former faith had had upon him. When the preacher finished, the man rose, saying to himself: "I am now satisfied. I don't need to stay in Amoy any longer. I am con-

A BARBER.

vinced of the truth of Christianity, and henceforth that is my faith." He travelled home rejoicing.

Almost the very first act when he got there was to gather the thirty idols and destroy them. Some were made of clay; these he smashed into a thousand pieces. Others were made of wood, and these he chopped into bits, and burnt in the fire. When his father came in from the fields and saw the destruction of the idols, he was horrified. What impious hands had dared to commit such an act of sacrilege? He absolutely trembled with fear, for he was convinced that some terrible judgment would come upon the family in consequence. When he found that it was his son, he rushed at him, and would have laid violent hands upon him, but that he fled and got out of his way, and for fully two years he never ventured to be in the same room with his father. Ultimately the whole family became Christian, and the son is to-day one of the most earnest and successful preachers we have, and presides over a church with a membership of one hundred and three persons, and an inquirers' class of one hundred and fifty.

For eight years the Gospel was preached from this house in the suburbs, and converts from heathenism were baptized there, till it became too small to accommodate the congregation that met for worship every Sunday. Every effort had failed to get into the city. The influence of the scholars and leading men had so far prevailed that no suitable building in it could be rented. At last the time came when the church was to enter it, not to occupy an insignificant position in some back street, but one of the finest and best known places in the city. An opium smoker, driven by his need for money, offered a piece of land for sale. His title deeds were examined and found to be satisfactory. The only difficulty about at once purchasing it, was the fact that it was in such a prominent place in the town that it was felt sure that the sternest and bitterest opposition would be made if the Christians attempted to build a church on it. It was in close proximity to the temple of the city god. Every walled town in China has its city god, that is supposed to control the spiritual affairs of the people, just as the chief mandarin does the secular. During the years that the Christians had been preaching, this conviction had been growing in the minds of the heathen, that wherever Christianity came the idols lost their power. Now this plot of land was only a few yards across the road from the entrance to the temple. The church when built would stand directly opposite to it. The Christians would be seen from its doors gathering for worship, and the sound of their singing would be heard inside it, and reach the very ears of the god. Not only would there be an uproar in any attempt to build, there would also be a very serious danger to the persons of the Christians. Such a possibility as this, however, never for a moment caused them to swerve from their desire to have this particular piece of ground bought. Whatever risk there might be, they were prepared to meet it. It was the very place, they reasoned, where the church ought to be built. Across the way was the heathen temple where men from all the region round, and even the mandarins in their official robes, at stated times came to worship. It was only right that close by should be the temple of the true God, where men might get the comfort and deliverance that were not to be obtained in the other.

They had been praying for years for a site, they said, and now that God had answered them beyond their highest expectation, were they to reject it because of the possibility of danger? Never. The land was accordingly bought by Mr. Stronach, and the builder at once commenced his work.

The excitement in the town was immense. Meetings of the literati were held, and threats fierce and terrible were uttered. The masses took up the cry of their leaders, and they vowed that no Christian church should desecrate their city; still no one took any active steps to interfere with the workmen. The building meanwhile went steadily up, foot by foot. The Christians had meetings for special prayer for help in this emergency, and still the church rose higher and higher, till finally the roof was completed, and it did seem as though the threats and mutterings of the scholars and the people were to result in nothing. God, however, had determined to answer the cry of his people in a more thorough way than by the mere preservation of the building. Soon after the roof had been put on, a crowd one day suddenly collected in a very mysterious and yet business-like manner in front of the church. It was a suspicious looking crowd, and it had mischief in its looks. A crowd in China soon begets a larger one. The stream of people passing along the great highway stopped in wonder, and then joined it. The opium smokers and gamblers from their low dens hurried along with eager, dissipated looks to join the crowd, for they had hopes of plunder that would fill their pipes with opium, or that would give them the means of a night's carouse. The thieves and men who got their living by their wits heard of the gathering of the storm with delight, and soon their voices were heard in the crowd protesting against the invasion of their city by the Christians, and of the insult to their great god over the way. A mob does not stand idle long. The instinct of order that is so deeply implanted in the mind of the Chinese restrained it for some time from actual violence; but the disorderly elements that kept continually flowing into it aroused the passions of the rest, till at last in a moment of frenzy the mob surged into the building, and the work of destruction began. Everything they could lay their hands on disappeared as if by magic. Then bands of eager, desperate men began to tear the church to pieces. The tiles on the roof and the beams on which they rested were carried off, and even the very pavement of the floor was torn up in some places. Doors moved away as if instinct with life, and hurried down by-streets, and along narrow alley ways till they finally vanished from sight. Just at this juncture, when the building was rapidly dissolving, a police force appeared upon the scene, and the crowd of opium smokers, and thieves, and gamblers instantly melted away before it.

A few days after this I visited the city, and had an interview with the mandarin. He was a very agreeable old gentleman, and received me in a very kind and cordial manner. After a little conversation, he promised to repair all the damage done to the building, and to restore it to me as good as it was before the outbreak. "And when we get into it," I asked him, " will you protect us, and will you restrain the scholars and the people from again molesting us?

Turning to me with a pleasant smile, he said : "I'll protect you as long as I am in office here, and if any one dares to lift a finger against you, just inform me, and I'll know where to find him." God had answered the prayer of His church by giving it a position in the town that has never been disturbed from that day to this. The old man faithfully kept his word, and stood our friend as long as he lived; and when he died a few years afterwards there was none that more sincerely mourned his death than the Christians.

Thirteen years have passed away since we got a footing in the town. The church has largely grown since then, and has been self-supporting for many years. Several years ago, a new church had to be built to accommodate the greatly increased numbers, whilst the old one has since been used as a school, etc. The last Sunday I spent with the Christians was a memorable one. The church was crowded with a very large assembly, so that the heathen had to stand in groups around the doors as there was no room for them inside. An ordination service was being held, and two native ministers and myself were ordaining a young man as pastor over this large and united church. The choice of the people had been unanimous, and the one feature in his character that had drawn every heart to him was his godliness. He was not an eloquent preacher, neither was he distinguished for his great learning. His fame had gone throughout the churches as one that lived near God, and one in whom the Spirit of God dwelt; and this church desired to have such a man for their pastor. As I looked over the great assemblage before me my heart was deeply moved. Before me I saw old men that had passed the best years of their life in the service of idolatry, with the new light that the Gospel sheds, and gleams of the coming glory on their faces. Young men were there, too, bright and happy looking, because of the new purpose and new hopes that had come into their lives. The heathen look had vanished, and in its place had come such a one as only a belief in Christ can infuse into a man's face.

It was a splendid gathering, and a marvellous one too. It was not a congregation of Christians that had been transplanted from some other place to show the people of this city how God should be worshipped. Every man and woman there had been gathered out of heathen homes from the region around. The opium dens, and the gambling houses, and the abodes of vice had all contributed to swell the number. Rakes and profligates, and men of abandoned character, whom no power in all China could influence for good, touched by a Divine hand, that was slowly effacing the scars of their old life, and that was putting in the first touches of the new image, that was to be the reflection of Christ's own in the future, were conspicuous in it. It was an assemblage that the angels in heaven might rejoice over, for in it was the promise of the new forces that God was going to employ for the conversion of the county to Himself.

Whilst the Gospel was being preached from the miserable house in the suburbs, which was to culminate in this beautiful church in the city, and the "Great Mother" was still looking lovingly down upon the church that was growing at her foot, a remarkable conversion took place of a man who was to play no mean part in the spread of the truth in this county.

His home was in one of the most beautiful and romantic places in all the region round. It was situated in a village that lay nestled under the shadow of the hills. To get to it one had to climb mountains, and descend along the sides of deep ravines by narrow and precipitous paths, and cross rugged passes where travelling was a weariness and a pain. One of these latter was exceedingly beautiful, and was called the "Sunlit Pass." It was so named because, from its peculiar conformation, the sun shone upon it during nearly the whole of the day. In the early morning, when the sun had risen just above the eastern mountains, his rays flashed from peak to peak, and streamed along the slopes of the hills, and chased away the shadows in the deep ravines that furrowed their sides, and finally lit up the stream that rushed and tumbled in foam over the black rocks hundreds of feet below. In the afternoon, when the sun began to climb down towards the mountains on the west, still the pass was ablaze with light, and the giant peaks stood bathed in a flood of glory, reaching away up in the blue sky, as though their aim was to touch the heavens with their summits. The rays that played upon the lower hills, and put out the shadows from the valleys and ravines, and that gleamed upon the roaring stream below, were not the reflection of those that flashed about those mighty peaks, they came straight from the fiery faced sun, that daily showed his power in this beautiful pass. I have never passed through it without feeling myself entranced with the grandeur of the scene. I take my stand in the centre of it. The mountains are marshalled around me, and lofty peaks towering up from them look down upon me in solemn majesty. No sound but the music of the stream and the indescribable harmonies of nature break the silence. As I look up, it seems as though those mighty forms are instinct with life, and by and by they will speak to me. Unconsciously to myself the idea gets more hold upon me, and I wait expectantly for voices that shall be a revelation and a strength to me when I again mingle in the human stream beyond the pass.

In this village, in the valley at the head of the Sunlit Pass, lived a small farmer, of the name of Ting. He was exceedingly poor. His father had been a gambler, and during his lifetime had sold many of his fields, and even part of the ancestral home to pay his debts of honour. The consequence was that it was a constant struggle with Ting to provide for the daily needs of his family. The fields that his father had not sold were not enough for this, so he had to meet the deficiency by cutting down the brushwood, and the smaller pine trees on the hillside, and selling them for firewood in a market town some ten miles distant. Ting was a man of great energy, and of indomitable will, and when he had set his mind upon anything, nothing in the world could make him swerve from his purpose. His face has always been a study to me. Usually it is a very pleasant one, and there is a tender, womanly smile upon it, that gives one the impression that there is not much force of character behind it. A little further study of it reveals the fact that the conclusion we have arrived at is a mistaken one. As long as there is nothing special being discussed, and the face is in repose, it seems to be that of an ordinary good-tempered man, but let a difference arise, and a marvellous change at once passes over it. Every feature seems to fall into an attitude of defiance; the lines around the mouth become contracted, and the head is slightly poised on one side, whilst the smile retreats into the background of the face, and seems like the vanishing glory of the setting sun on the mountains in the far-off distance.

One day he had carried his firewood to the market town by the sea-side, and after standing long in the market place, had succeeded in disposing of it. He was winding his way through the streets on his return home, when he noticed a crowd gathered by the roadside listening to a man who was addressing them. He drew near to see what was the matter, when he heard the speaker say: "All the idols in China are false." He was startled. Never had such words been uttered in his hearing before. His first impulse was to resent what the preacher said. "That is not true," he reasoned with himself. "I have worshipped the idols all my life, and my father and mother too before me." Every man and woman, moreover, in his village looked to them for protection, he thought, and no shadow of a doubt had ever been expressed regarding their ability to help men. He began to feel indignant, but still the preacher went on with his argument. He showed how the idols were the source of sorrow and misery to the country, and how in the great crises of human life they were absolutely helpless to comfort or relieve. The speaker's facts coincided with his own experience. The touches of human life that were given in his discourse recalled many a sad event in his own history, and unconsciously to himself a mighty revolution was going on in his mind, that would drive the idols for ever from his heart, and lead him to the worship of the true God. He still stands on the edge of the crowd listening in rapt attention to the words of the preacher. The tramp of men with heavy burdens on their shoulders, and the loud excited tones of men wrangling about the prices of their goods, and the confused noise and uproar of the busy, crowded market fall unheeded upon his ears, for he is listening to truths that are moving his heart as it has never been touched before.

But he feels he must return home. The day is swiftly passing away, and the evening shadows are beginning to lengthen. He has a long walk before him, along a weary painful road to travel too; besides, it is not very safe to be amongst the mountains after dark, as there are tigers upon them. All the journey home, he cannot get the words of the preacher out of his mind. He passes along the plain, and through the villages that dot it; he ascends the mountains, and enters the Sunlit Pass out of which the light has nearly all faded, and he winds his way by the mountain stream and reaches his own village, but still the words, "All the idols in China are false," ring in his ears. He will never get them out of his heart as long as he lives.

When he entered his home, and the usual greetings had passed between him and his family, he said to his mother: "Mother, I have had a wonderful experience to-day. I heard a man declare to a large crowd in the market town that all the idols in China are false. "My son," she quickly replied, "the man that says that is mad. Haven't we worshipped them all our life, and our fathers before us, and the people of all this region, and if they are false, who then has guarded and protected us? We know of no power beside theirs." "Yes, I know that," he slowly and thoughtfully answered, "but I have been thinking all the way home this evening, if the idols can really protect us, why are we so poor? It is a daily struggle with us all for life. See how poorly clad you are, and what miserable food you have to eat. I should like to care for you better, but I cannot, and it seems as though we get poorer and poorer. This cannot surely be the result of the displeasure of the idols, for we make our regular offerings to them, and we spend money on them that is taken out of our very life's blood. "My son," the mother cried out in agony, "don't say such things. You will anger the gods, and some dire calamity will fall upon our home. If you talk this way you will soon be as bad as the man you heard to-day."

The son became silent, but his thoughts were all the more busy. Next Sunday morning, just before dawn, he is on his way to the church in the village that lies at the foot of the "Great Mother." His heart is sadly agitated, and he cannot rest. He has so many questions to ask, and so many perplexities to unravel. He spends the day with the Christians, who receive him with loving affection, so very different from what a heathen company would have done. His doubts and anxieties vanish as they tell him of God, the loving Father, who has created all things, and knows the hearts and thoughts of every living creature. Never in his wildest dreams regarding supernatural beings has he ever thought of such an one as this. He had feared and he had dreaded the unseen powers, and he had made many offerings to them to avert their anger, and induce them to look kindly upon him, but to-day he hears of One who loves him. His heart is satisfied.

A few weeks pass by and he is received into the church, and no truer man, or more valiant defender of the truth, ever made his confession of faith in Christ in the county than he. Years have elapsed since then, and there is to-day a flourishing self-supporting church in his village, whose influence is felt beyond the hills that encircle it, and further than the Sunlit Pass, and right away amongst the valleys of the neighbouring county of the "Pleasure Ground of the Fairies."

Twenty-four years have come and gone since the miserable little opium smoker and gambler left his home to retrieve his fortunes in Amoy. The Gospel that was brought back by him to his native village, has spread through the county till now there are eleven churches in it, nine of which are self-supporting, one partially so, and another that is assisted by the voluntary contributions of one of the native churches in Amoy. Only one out of the eleven has to have the salary of its preacher supplemented by the funds that come from England.

It may be asked here what is the peculiar charm about the Gospel that has attracted so many in this poor county to believe in it. I can answer unhesitatingly that it is Christ and Him crucified. I remember one day questioning a large number of candidates just previous to their being baptized.

Amongst them were two scholars, a father and his son. For several years the former had been an opium smoker, but life seemed to flow on pretty smoothly, till one day to his horror he discovered that his son had taken to the pipe. He was in great distress, for he knew that sorrow and misery now lay before his son. With the heroic stoicism of the Chinese he was prepared to pay the penalty for his wrong, but he could not endure to think of the young life being brought so early within the influence of a vice that would ruin and destroy it. He appealed to him to smoke no more, but his words were paralyzed by his own bad example. He then called upon a Christian in the village, and entreated him to use his influence to save his son. The young fellow, however, resisted all attempts to make him abandon the pipe. Seeing that all his arguments were making no impression, as a last resort he adopted a ruse by which he hoped to touch him. Coming to his house one day, he said to him: "I have spent a great deal of time in endeavouring to get you to give up opium. I have been making a great mistake in this, for I have discovered that you are a man of such a weak character, and so wanting in energy, that it is impossible for you ever to be cured. There is no hope for you, and so I have come to tell you that I am not going to waste my time any more on you. You are not worth it."

The young fellow sat with congested eyes looking at him whilst he was making these remarks, and was so utterly taken aback by his rudeness, that he had not a word to say in reply. After he had gone out, he said to himself: "Weak character, indeed! Cannot be cured, forsooth! I'll show him that I am a stronger man than he believes me to be, and that I have strength of will enough to give up the opium if I like." The bait had taken. His pride and self-respect were touched, and from that instant he began gradually to free himself from the fascination of the opium pipe. His father was delighted, and to encourage his son, began to imitate his example, whilst at the same time he became a regular attendant at our religious services. There he found such comfort and strength in the terrible struggle with opium, that he induced his son to accompany him, and in process of time they were both free men.

The old man had an exceedingly intelligent face, for it had been sharpened by many years of thought and study. His eyes were black and brilliant, and when he became excited they flashed as though the fires of youth still burned brightly in his breast. The haughty look, however, which is a general characteristic of the Chinese scholar, had vanished. The very position, indeed, that he occupied that day showed what a mighty change had come over him. Close beside him were several uneducated men and women that were going to make their confession of Christ. He did not resent being placed by their side, nor his having to tell the story of his conversion in the presence of his heathen countrymen, that crowded into the building to watch the proceedings. When I asked the old man what it was that gave him peace, he answered at once that it was the fact that Christ had died upon the cross for him, and had washed away his sins in His precious blood. He did not speak of the delivery from opium that had come to himself and his son as the cause of his happiness. He found it in the cross of Christ. It was the same with the son, a sturdy wide-awake young fellow, brimming over with life and energy, and when I turned to the rest, I found that in every case the central thought in the confession both of men and women, was the same as his. The stories that I heard that day of changed lives, and beautiful hopes, and purposes to live a better life, were all inspired by the Cross, and as I looked upon the faces before me, and then to those of the heathen that filled up the background of the congregation, I felt that this was to be the great power that was to elevate China, and place her high amongst the Christian nations of the world.

CHAPTER VIII.

PHO-LAM.

TWENTY-SIX years have passed by since Mr. Stronach first arrived in Amoy to establish a mission there. The work has prospered more or less in every direction. Christianity has become a power in the town, as two large self-supporting churches attest. The churches in the Chiang-Chiu and Koan-Khau districts are flourishing, and even in the far-off county of Gracious Peace there are already indications that Christianity will one day be a mighty factor in the life of that poor county. In the year 1870, it was again determined to take another step in advance, and to begin work in an entirely new district, in a market town of great importance some thirty miles from Amoy, up the North River, named Pho-lam. The situation of this place is a very picturesque one. Immediately beyond it rises a range of mountains, diversified by many a lofty peak that stretch away into the distance, until they lose themselves amidst the clouds which they seem to be holding up. In front of it flows the river, which has but recently emerged from the hills. A while ago it was a foaming torrent, as it dashed through the mighty gorges, and curled in great eddies where sudden reefs lay, or dashed itself into spray upon the rocks that rose above its surface, in the very channel through which it was madly racing to the plains below. The boatmen, who have but recently been whirled down its numerous rapids and have come in excited as if after a mad race, can hardly recognise the river, as it placidly flows in gentle, decorous manner past the town.

Behind Pho-lam, and away on the opposite bank of the river, stretches the great plain of Chiang-Chiu. It is dotted with countless villages and fields of rice; and endless clumps of sugar-cane indicate that the people of this highly favoured region are prosperous and well-to-do.

Pho-lam was a great trade centre. The teas that were then sent from Amoy to America all came down the river, and had to be transhipped here. Great rafts of timber, too, were shot down the rapids, and reposed alongside the town as quietly and as circumspectly as though they had never gone through any such wild experience. Boats packed to overflowing with packages of paper made from the bamboos that grew in rich luxuriance on the mountain sides and in the valleys, came in daily to be sent down to Amoy, from whence they were despatched in steamers along the coast, and away to Singapore and Manilla. Beside all this, there was a great fair held in the place every fifth day, when the farmers brought their produce, and buyers and sellers from far and near crowded the streets. It struck me that it would be a capital centre for missionary work. The Gospel could be here preached to the representatives of almost every village in the plain, as well as to men from the towns that lay beyond those rapids, and behind the great

A PAGODA.

mountains that frowned between us and the unknown country at their back. There was just one discouraging feature in the case—the men of Pho-lam had an evil reputation. They were notorious gamblers and opium smokers. The place abounded with houses for both purposes, and it did seem a hopeless task to build up a Christian church in such a town, and with such materials.

But let us take a ramble through its streets, and see what is the character of the place where we are going to commence our new work. It is fair day, and crowds have come in from regions far and near. How busy the town is! Farmers are carrying the produce of their farms on their shoulders to the market places. Men with great baskets of oranges from the neighbouring orange groves come panting along. Large numbers of young fellows saunter about with open mouths, greatly enjoying the sights of the fair. They have come in from remote villages to see the fun, and to break the everlasting monotony of country life. Huge delight is pictured on their faces, and their eyes sparkle as they move slowly amongst the ever increasing crowd of men. Here, in a convenient opening from the main street, is the world-wide show of Punch and Judy, acting almost precisely as they used to do when I was a boy, and when I spent many a delicious hour in watching the comedies and tragedies of that inimitable acting. The rustics are entranced. Broad grins overspread their faces, and exclamations of delight show how their sense of the comical has been touched. But let us hasten on, for further down the street there is a sound of high jinks and revelry. The sounds of cymbals noisily clashing, and the shrill music of clarionets, and the waves of laughter that come up on the breeze, show there is some uproarious fun going on. We find that it is a comedy that is being acted by a party of actors, and the crowd is being convulsed by the jokes and comical antics of certain of the players. When they find a foreigner amongst their audience every eye is turned upon me. The actors in the midst of their funniest bits gaze at me. The man with the cymbals is just as furious as ever when some great joke has been made, but his eye is fixed on me. As the men move about the stage representing some scene in life, they linger on the side near me and have a prolonged stare at me. It is becoming embarrassing to have so many eyes upon me, so I move away, amidst the broad grins of the players; and again the clarionet gives forth its shrillest sounds, and the rattle of the drum becomes more rapid and prolonged, and once more the sound of laughter floats upon the air, and reaches us after we have lost sight of the merry gathering. The shops to-day are all busy, for customers crowd into them during the busiest hours of the fair. But how is it that, interspersed amongst them, there are so many houses with bamboo screens hanging in front of the open doors? Let us enter one, for it is not a private house. It is an opium den. We put the screen aside, and come into a dimly lighted room, with a broad bench running round the sides of it. Little lamps are placed at various intervals, and men are reclining beside them. Some are asleep, and most ghastly do they look with their haggard, opium-hued faces. They are stretched on their backs, and they seem as if they were corpses. They don't appear like men whose spirits are wandering in fairy land, and are entranced with gorgeous scenes of beauty, such as the opium smoker is said to enjoy. Others, again, are busy manipulating the opium, and are slowly inserting tiny bits into their narrow pipes. A whiff or two and the bits are exhausted, when they renew the process, and will continue to do so till they doze off, and are in the land of dreams like the rest. They look at me with surprise, as a foreigner is about the last man they expect to see amongst them. One man smiles at me, and whilst he is melting the tiny piece of opium over the flame, on the end of something very like a knitting-needle, he says, giving the needle a jerk towards me: "This comes from your country, doesn't it?" I feel distressed, for I know he does but express the common opinion that all opium comes from England. But this opium den is an unsavoury place to be in. The close, horrid smell, the ghastly figures ranged along the benches, and the sense of being in the midst of some of the very lowest of the population, are oppressive. We hear the sounds of voices outside, and we see the rays of the bright sun shining upon the bamboo mat, and we rush out of the dim, fetid place, with a sense of deliverance, into the open air. We walk along as quickly as the crowd will let us, just to get away from the street, and if possible, from the very thoughts associated with it. By and by we observe a shop, quite open to the street, in which are groups of men gathered round tables, engaged in some absorbing occupation. The crowd surges by. Men in loud tones discuss market prices. Men in excited voices come almost to the point of serious altercation over some disputed piece of business. But these groups hear nothing. They are gamblers. They are forbidden by law to gamble, and there are penalties for the infraction of the law. Only a few yards away there is a mandarin's court. You wonder how they dare gamble so near him! The fact is, a man may break almost any law he chooses if he will only pay for the liberty of doing so. The policeman may be standing by watching the gamblers, but he does not perceive that they are gambling. "They are a few friends met for an innocent social amusement, or they are assembled for the serious study of their sacred classics, or they are engaged in the discussion of some deep metaphysical subject:" so he will report to his superior, for the gamblers have bribed him, and they rely upon him to screen them from trouble. Look at the men, how engrossed they are in the cards they are holding in their hands! There is a smile of satisfaction on the faces of the winners, and a dogged, unhappy look, on those that have been unlucky. Loud wrangling now and again takes place at some piece of unfairness. Some of these men have a desperate look about them. They are professed gamblers. Others are evidently farmers' sons, that have come in from their quiet villages to have a time of dissipation. They are no match for the former, and they will lose every cash they possess. At last the game is over, and the losers have to pay. There is a tremendous row, and the regular gamblers with fiendish faces and violent gestures are pouring forth the vials of their wrath on one unfortunate who dared to play the last game though he had no money. He is stoutly protesting that he will bring the money to-morrow, and pay them all he owes them, but they refuse to consent. All of a sudden a rush is made at him. His arms are pinioned by some of the low browed ruffians, and in an instant his coat is stripped from his back, and he is hurled into the street. The policeman stands by with a bland smile. You wonder he does not rush in and stop the fray. Oh no, there is no disturbance whatever. It is merely a rather heated discussion upon the first principles of Heaven, or on the Five Constant Virtues as propounded in the Divine works of the great Confucius. He has been properly feed by the owner of the establishment, and he is bound to be blind to any of the incidents that may take place in connection with the business. No one in fact interferes in any way with the summary method of doing justice that these gamblers have. The conscience of the crowd that look on is not at all outraged by it, and even the man himself tacitly acknowledges that the rough way in which he has been treated is not unjust. He slinks away as fast as he can, and is soon lost to sight amidst the crowd.

It was fair day when we arrived at Pho-lam. When we got opposite the town, the approaches were so blocked up by the crowds of boats that anchored off it, that we experienced great difficulty in landing. When we at last got on shore, we found ourselves amidst a great surging mass of people, that were pressing eagerly to see the foreigner. Probably not any of them had ever seen one before. Vague rumours had come up the river about the existence of men from the west, who were residing in Amoy, but here to-day was one of them in their very midst and with whom they could converse, for he knew their own language. When we got into the church, it was instantly filled to overflowing by a motley crowd, all anxious to have a good look at the foreigner that had come to preach his strange doctrines in the town. The scene before us was an impressive one, and in some respects a weird one. If there could have been a Hogarth amongst us to have portrayed the various faces there, he could have produced a picture that would have immortalized him. There were farmers and shopkeepers, and opium smokers with pale and haggard faces, dyed with the unfading hue that opium stamps upon it; and conspicuous, too, were the gamblers, with the hungry look in their eyes and restless movement of their fingers, that seemed perpetually to be manipulating invisible cards, or grasping the dice ready for a throw. Not one of the mass before us knew anything of God. If each had been asked, who made the mountains outside that were ablaze with glory, or the river that flowed by their town, not one could have told. There was no one, moreover, whose life would have borne inspection. One short inquiry into the history of any of them, and we should have shrunk back, lest our thoughts should be contaminated by the sight that would have been revealed to us.

The babel of voices soon became hushed, and the exclamations of wonder and surprise gradually died away, as we proceeded to tell them of the great Father and His eternal love. We spoke to them of Christ, of His great sacrifice, and how He came to redeem men from their sins and their vices. As we dwelt on this topic, the crowd became rapt in their attention. Every eye was fixed on us. The great sun flashed and blazed in the street outside, and his beams played about the doors, and fell upon the faces of the gamblers and opium smokers, and made them look ghastly; but they thought not of this, for the Divine story was touching their hearts, and proving that its ancient power was as potent as ever.

After we had been speaking some time, a man came quickly from the crowd where he had been standing, and kneeling down before me, began knocking his head upon the ground. I at once took him by the arm and told him to get up at once. With some little difficulty I got him on his feet, the crowd the meanwhile looking on with amazement. I then asked him what he wanted. He told me that he had been deeply moved by what he had just heard. "I have been an opium smoker," he said, "for many years. I am a complete slave to the habit, and I feel that I have no power to help myself, and no one around me can. You spoke of the power of God to save me. Can you do anything to deliver me?" And as he said these words, he was about to precipitate himself again before me. I looked at him steadily whilst he was talking. His face had a terribly dissipated look about it. Vice had left its impress upon it, and so it had a coarse, sensual look, as though it had been dragged through the very slough of wickedness all his life. His clothes were shabby in the extreme. They were greasy and torn. He was about the very last man in all that fair that day I should have selected to become the first stone in the spiritual temple that God was going to build in that town of Pho-lam. As I looked at him, my faith in the man waned. These opium smokers are such liars, and so exceedingly difficult to cure, that I considered his case absolutely hopeless. I said to him: "If you are in earnest, of course you can be saved. Christ can save worse men than you are. Are you really in earnest, though? Remember, the first thing you will have to do is to give up your opium. Are you prepared for that?" "I am," he said; "try me." I at once assured him that if he really had made up his mind to consent to this, I would help him to the very utmost of my ability, and that I would stand by him to the very last. I told him he must come every day and study the life of Christ, and be instructed in truths that would strengthen him for the struggle that he was now going to have with opium and his old vices. He readily assented to this, and ere long a marvellous change was seen in him. The sallow, ghastly look in his face disappeared, and the slightest suspicion of colour gave it a more healthy hue. His clothes, too, were more respectable, and he lost the slouching gait that was but an outcome of the life he used to lead. He at once began to work, and soon his steady life and his quiet, unassuming manners drew customers to the little shop he had opened. His brother, who to save himself from being dragged down to his own level, had been compelled to turn him on to the streets, looked on with perfect amazement at the transformation. What mysterious power had touched his brother! He could not understand it, so he came to the church to get the explanation; and he was so moved by the story of the Cross that had converted his brother, that he gave up idolatry, and with his whole family became Christians. One of his sons was a fine manly young fellow, who became such an earnest worker in the church that he was elected a deacon, which office he has held for years, being highly esteemed for his godly, consistent life. The old opium smoker has been for years one of the pillars of the church, and has exercised a very powerful influence over the young men of it. The tragedies of his own life, and the terrible scenes through which he has passed, enable him to speak with a pathos and a power to them that help them to resist the temptations that still abound in that market town. One would never dream, as he sits reading his large print Bible, that he was once the low dissipated character, such as we can see in the opium dens to-day. His face is now pleasant to look at. The Gospel has long ago taken the fierce, bad look out of his eyes, and has made his manners gentle and loving. I delight to sit and gaze at the old man, for he is a standing miracle to me, and I never look at him without having instantly before me the terrible picture of what he was when I first saw him. There was no power in China, or in all the world, that could have changed him into the man that he is to-day, excepting the Gospel of our Lord and Saviour Jesus Christ.

The next conspicuous character that appears amongst the early Christians of Pho-lam was a very different kind of person from the opium smoker. He was a tall, elderly man, thoughtful looking, and with a dignified and serious manner. He was evidently in a good position in society, as I could see by the way he dressed. In our discussions with him regarding the Christian religion, there were some questions that were evidently a perplexity to him, and so we had patiently to discuss with him until his difficulties were removed. We found that by profession he was a geomancer, and one of the most noted in all that region. Geomancy is a system that has a tremendous hold upon all classes of society, and is interwoven with the most cherished beliefs and the social life of rich and poor. It is a popular and deep-seated conviction that the place where the dead are buried has a great deal to do with the fortunes not only of those that are laid in the grave, but also of the relatives that are still alive. This superstition goes by the name of "wind and water." The air is supposed to be filled with good and bad influences, that are always bringing either prosperity or misfortune to mankind. The mountains and the valleys have concealed within them the mysterious dragons that have the power, when properly utilized, of bringing untold wealth and honours into a family. The selection of a site, therefore, is a matter of the greatest importance, and very often rich men will lie unburied for months, and even years, because of the difficulty of securing a piece of ground that will meet all the laws of geomancy. There is a class of men who spend their lives in the study of these, and who are employed by those who can afford it to select the lucky spots for their deceased relatives. When a thoroughly good place has been obtained, then, it is believed, business will begin to prosper, sons will be born in rapid succession in the family, the boys will in time pass their examinations and become mandarins, and the father and the mother will live to a good old age, surrounded by their children and their grand-children. If, however, the geomancer has been mistaken as to the lie of the dragon, or to the evil influences that come swirling round some mountain peak and, unconsciously to him, have neutralized the good ones that, according to all the laws of geomancy, ought to be blowing over the ground, then dire disasters will be the result. The mother, for example is buried in it. Not long after, there is a tremendous fall in the market, and certain goods have to be sold at a ruinous price, that seriously affects the fortunes of the family. Trade never comes back again to the firm, and customers go to others for their purchases. One of the little ones is playing about in the courtyard and falls into the open well and is drowned; one of the daughters suddenly falls ill a few days before her marriage, and after a severe attack of fever is carried off. The eldest son, who has been remarkably steady before, begins to associate with evil companions; he becomes an opium smoker, and a rake; he goes abroad like the prodigal son, but never returns as he did, and rumours by and by reach the old home that he has ended his life a dissipated, ruined spend-thrift. All these disasters are traced to the evil influences that are moaning and sighing over the mother's grave on the lonely hill-side, and to the baneful working of the dragon that has been offended by some disregard of laws that affected its dignity or its comfort.

After long discussions with him in regard to Christianity, he one day said: " Now I am convinced of the truth of your religion, I want you to baptize me, for I wish to be a Christian." "Before I can baptize you," I replied, "you will have to give up your profession." This statement of mine seemed to completely stagger him. I remember well, how he drew himself up in a stately dignified manner, and then, with his whole soul put into his face, he leaned eagerly over to me, and with tremendous emphasis in his voice, he said : " Then you wish me to die ? " I assured him that I did not, but he was too impressed with the demand that I had made upon him to heed my disclaimer. "You know," he continued, "I am an old man now. I have made a good deal of money by my profession, and I have lived very comfortably, but I have saved nothing. I have been kind to my poor relatives, and even now I have a nephew that I am supporting in the town. You very calmly tell me to give up my profession, but what am I to do for a living, for beyond that I have no resources to fall back upon ? " I assured him of my intense sympathy with him, and that I did not wish him to die. " I want you to live," I said, " and not die. I want you, with all your ability, and knowledge of the people here, to be a member of this church, so that you may be a power on the side of Christ. You must go away and pray over the matter. You are now called upon to make a great sacrifice, and you need Divine strength to help you. Go home and think over the matter, and ask God to give you the purpose and the strength to carry you through this great trial." He went away very soberly and very solemnly, with the shadow of the coming sorrow on his face. As he passed out into the street my heart followed after him. It ached for him. Will he come back again ? He has come up to the very door of the kingdom, one step more and he will be inside ; and now, after all our discussions and our rejoicing over his confession of

Christ, he seems to be slipping out of our grasp. He has gone out into the darkness to study amidst his heathen surroundings this fundamental law of Christ's kingdom, that if a man would be a follower of Christ, he must be prepared to give up all for love of Him, that in this great surrender Christ may be able to give him back more than a hundred-fold more than he has given up for Him. He has to face this, not as a beautiful theory, but as a stern practical truth. The question he has now to decide is whether, in obedience to One whom he has known for but a few months, he is willing to abandon a mode of livelihood upon which he depends for his very subsistence, and trust to Him for his daily food. Surely this is a tremendous question to settle, especially for a man who has just emerged out of heathenism, with none of the long experiences that help the Christian to make great sacrifices. After a severe mental conflict he returned to tell us his story. As I caught sight of his face, I knew what the result was, and my heart leaped for joy. "It is all settled, Mr. Macgowan," he said to me, "but it has been after a terrible struggle. The Lord has helped me to a decision, and now I shall nevermore have anything to do with geomancy as long as I live. But it has been no easy matter, you know;" and he bent his head towards me as he said this in a lowered voice, and a troubled look came over his face, as though he were again going through the dread ordeal. "It is like cutting off my right arm," he said; and now there was a stern look upon his face, and suiting the action to the word he held up high his arm, and seemed to be cutting it off with an imaginary knife. "But never mind," he continued, " I am now old, and soon the sun will set behind the western mountains, and ere long I shall be with God, and it matters little what I have to suffer here." As the old man went on talking, and his face became illumined with the glow that this great sacrifice had shed upon it, I looked upon him with intense admiration. He was to me a grander hero than all the heroes of romance, whose names have sparkled in ballad and in story. His resolution was faithfully kept, though for some months he had to suffer considerable privations. He became a doctor, and travelled round the country selling medicines. It was a long time before his reputation became so far established that he could gain enough to meet all the requirements of his daily life. I never heard him complain, or express a single regret at the course he had taken, neither did he ever hint that he had made any special sacrifice for his faith. He always spoke of the peace of mind he had obtained, and the joy and comfort God had given him. The people in the region around were amazed that he, so famous a geomancer, should give up his profession. They could not conceive why a man in his position should give up a business that was bringing him in so much money, simply because he believed in a certain set of doctrines taught him by the foreigners. There must be some foul play, or enchantment, they argued, to make him act in such a mad, unreasonable fashion. Not all the gods in China, nor all the teachings of their Divine sages, could have moved a Chinaman to do what he had done. They shook their heads, and looked in wonder at each other, and finally put it down to some mysterious and unearthly fascination the foreigner possessed, and which they as good and loyal citizens should be careful to guard against. Many were the applications that he received to go on the hill-sides and point out the lucky places where the people might bury their dead; but he refused them all, though there were times when he sadly needed the money that they were ready to thrust upon him for his services.

The early growth of the Pho-lam church was rapid, and it soon began to acquire a reputation for earnestness and godliness that has clung to it to the present day. It was very fortunate in the character of its first converts. They were men who had profound faith in the Gospel, and their lives were generally so consistent that they made a deep impression on those that were subsequently baptized. God was to them a reality. He mingled in their lives. He gave them counsel in times of sickness and sorrow, and He was a comfort to them when they were oppressed by their heathen neighbours. It was beautiful to see how soon these men, that all their lives had been accustomed to dumb idols, realized the presence of a loving Father in all the details of their life. As the Church grew in numbers our anxieties and cares were proportionately increased. A missionary's duties are remarkably varied. They do not consist simply in standing in the front of some temple, or in a retired nook off some main street, and preaching to the crowds that gather round him. Neither do they consist in holding certain services with the Christians, or in baptizing converts. These are simple and delightful matters, and are to me the very poetry and romance of missionary life. His duties include a wide field beyond these, that often cause him much perplexity, and if he be of a sympathetic nature, much sorrow of heart. He has to be a veritable father to his people, and he has to listen to all their trials, and sorrow, and experiences, and to comfort them the best way he can. A man, for example, becomes a Christian. His wife, who happens to be the better man of the two, makes his life an utterly miserable one. Six days of the week he has no peace, and on the seventh, which he has been looking forward to as one of rest and enjoyment, which he will spend in the church, he finds his clothes locked up, and himself condemned to bed for the day. The poor man comes perhaps on the Monday with a long face to tell his grievance. It is a ludicrous one, and one has great difficulty in repressing one's mirth, for, unfortunately, the comical side will obtrude itself, though it is a very tragical one for him. We comfort him and tell him to be patient, and that in due time his annoyances will cease, and perhaps his wife become a devoted Christian with himself. One sturdy looking Chinaman, with the war look in his face, and an outstretched brawny arm, says: "If she were my wife I should soon settle her"; and he waves his hand in such a threatening way that we all know precisely what he means, and so I say: "No, no! we cannot allow that. That is not the way to gain a woman's heart, neither is it the method that Christianity permits us to employ." "Ah," he replies, with a dogged determined look in his face, "that is all very well for you English people, but it will never do in China. A man must rule in his own home. Your ladies are educated, and they have been brought up in Christian ways from their childhood. Ours have not, and if you don't rule them, they will think you are weak. They will then take the reins into their own hands, and then what will become of the authority of the husband?" It requires a good many lessons before the Divine idea in reference to women is learnt by such a man.

Or perhaps there has been a season of drought. There is no water in the wells, the grass is dried up, the rice in the fields has been scorched and withered, and the sweet potato vines are blanched and dying. The family are bearing it patiently, though you can see they are pinched; but they are proud, and they don't like to have their poverty exposed. You cannot stand by and see them dying by inches. You must devise with the church some means for relieving their distress. Or again, a preacher falls seriously ill. In a few days he is dead, and his wife, who loved him dearly, is so paralyzed by the shock that in the course of a week or so she is buried by his side. The three children that are left orphans are claimed by the relatives; but as they are all heathen and intend to bring them up as such, we decide to take the charge of them ourselves. This is a grave reponsibility, for they are all young, and it means long years of almost parental anxiety for the missionary who has the oversight of them. The church nobly takes its share of the onerous duty, but on him the chief burden falls. I remember one day, after having spent a delightful Sunday with a certain church, as the members were pressing around me to say good-bye before they left for their mountain homes, a woman with a child strapped to her back, with a sad and tearful face, stood before me. Her husband, who was a shy modest fellow, stood a little way off. "What is the matter with you?" I asked her. "Are you in sorrow?" for I was deeply moved by her look of distress. It seemed that they lived in a village some two or three miles away, and that they were the only Christians in it. The annual festival in honour of the village idol's birthday was soon to be held, and this Christian man had been chosen by the villagers to arrange for it, and preside over the religious services. He had protested against this, and had informed the leaders of the heathen party that, being a Christian, he absolutely refused to have anything to do with the festival. They had replied in vigorous, but far from polite, language that he must either comply or leave the village. They came to me to see if I could counsel them what to do. I was perplexed. To appeal to the mandarins was useless. They would give no assistance to a Christian. To endeavour to touch the hearts of the heathen by laying before them the hardships they would bring upon the family, was a hopeless task. I talked over the matter with the Christians. They shook their heads. The village was notorious for its lawlessness, they said, and they feared none, not even their mandarins. They had selected the Christian on purpose, just that they might be able to expel him from their midst, for they had come to the resolution that they would not tolerate a Christian in their village. We could only counsel them to remain firm, and commit their case to the Lord; and after they had been driven out we should then consider how we were to sympathize with them.

Such cases as these are but samples of the many ways in which the heart of the missionary is tried.

What renders it all the more distressing is that sometimes the trials are so severe that the faith of the Christian gives way, and he abandons his Christianity. The story of one of the members of this Church will illustrate what I mean. Bi was a native of a large village some three miles away from Pho-lam. He was an itinerant seller of pork, which he used to carry in two baskets slung from the ends of a bamboo pole, which rested on his shoulder. To sell this he had to rise very early in the morning. The dew-drops were still upon the grass, and the fiery face of the sun hidden behind the hills across the plains, when the sound of his conch shell, the emblem of his trade, could be heard as he passed from village to village with his meat. Those who wished to buy for the day would gather around his baskets, and amidst the sounds of laughter that echoed through the great banyan trees, they would make their choice. He was a merry fellow and full of joke and jest, that made him a universal favourite; and besides all this, there was no man in all the country side that could sing a song so well as he. His business led him on fair days to Pho-lam. Here he first listened to the preaching of the Gospel. It made a deep impression upon him, so that in the course of a month or two he had completely broken with idolatry, and became a professed disciple of Jesus. His father was exceedingly indignant at this, and so also were the elders of the village. These latter were specially concerned because Bi was indispensable in their idol processions. When once a year with banners waving and sounds of music the chief village idol was carried in procession to have its spiritual powers rekindled at the fane from whence the sacred fire on its own altar was first obtained, Bi was a most prominent man in it. The cymbals and the flutes were useless without his voice. He would sing some stirring popular ballad that would touch the hearts of his hearers, and the streaming crowd would pass on merrily, and the strains of music would rise more wildly, as his voice was heard rehearsing the wondrous deeds of some ancient hero. His loss was irreparable, for there was no voice now left that could move the hearts of the crowd, or kindle such enthusiasm as his; and besides, his own village would lose its proud pre-eminence over its neighbours. No more would crowds gather on the outskirts of the village, by which the procession passed so jauntily, to listen to the voice that was the chief charm in it. His father was exceedingly bitter against him, and formally complained of him to the village elders. At the same time he authorized them to use severe measures against him, in order to cure the madness which he declared had come over his son. Fortunately his wife remained neutral, for if she had taken sides against him then his life would indeed have been miserable. In the meantime Bi was becoming a great favourite with the Christians. He was a genial, kind-hearted fellow, and would put himself out to any extent to help any one in need. As a proof of their affection and faith in him, they elected him to be a deacon, the duties of which he fulfilled to the satisfaction of every one. This went on for about four years, but the misery of his village life had never ceased. Every time an idol procession was organized, he had to fly from his home, and remain in the church till the festival was over. About the end of that time his business began to fail; he had lost his old popularity amongst the heathen, for they looked upon him as a traitor not only to his gods, but also to his country. His conch shell sounded as usual, but neither it nor his merry laugh could bring out the customers. He became dejected, and lost heart. His father was as bitter as ever, and the elders were not one whit more reconciled to his loss than they were four years ago. Just at this time his father, accompanied by the leading men of the village, came to see him, and told him that if he did not obey him and take part in the next procession, he would be seized and put in a bag and thrown into the river. He knew that this was no idle threat. He had suffered four long years of persecution; his business had failed; everything about him looked dark, and so he gave way. He never went back to idolatry, and though he once more sang the ballads in the next procession, it was not in honour of the idols. In the course of a few months he became so unhappy, and so dissatisfied with himself, that he emigrated and went abroad, and all knowledge of him has been completely lost. He was greatly mourned by the Christians, who loved him dearly; and he is still remembered to the present day with the most kindly feelings by those who knew him best. Many years have elapsed since he left us; but my heart aches when I think of the generous, manly fellow, whose presence was always as sunshine in our midst.

The changes that have taken place since I first visited this market town have been marvellous. When we first reached it, there was not a single person that, as far as we knew, had ever heard the

Gospel. We did not find one that had any idea of what Christianity meant. The moral darkness of the town was dense; heathenism was universal, and vice was running riot in it. The Divine story of the Gospel was told in the midst of this impure life, and hearts were soon touched by its beauty and pathos. Men of heroic faith, who had to suffer much for their confession of Christ, came within His influence, and became the spiritual stones in the new temple. Some who were built in less heroic mould, faltered and failed under the tremendous strain to which their faith was put; and others, with nothing specially conspicuous about their life, have patiently carried out the Christian virtues in the midst of their heathen surroundings. Many other workers since then have preached with power in this place, and the region around, and have helped to build up the church that has been established here. The mountains still look down, as of old, upon the town with its gamblers and opium smokers; but they also look upon a Christian community that assemble here for worship, whilst on the river bank, and away across the plain, and at the foot of the distant hills, four other churches have been formed where men may learn the way of life.

CHAPTER IX.

CONFUCIANISM, AND THE RESULTS OF MISSIONARY WORK IN AMOY.

THE greatest name in China for the last two thousand years has been that of Confucius. Great kings, and statesmen, and warriors, and poets, and famous writers have arisen during that time, whose lives have been woven, as it were, into the warp and woof of the history of the country, and whose memories will never die out as long as China is a nation. There is not one, however, of that vast array whose brilliant deeds or words have flashed a glory upon the nation that can be compared with Confucius, the great sage of China. He stands pre-eminent as the man whose "virtue is equal to heaven and earth," and before whose shrine the ruler of three hundred millions of people yearly bows and worships as a god. The influence of Confucius touches every class of society, from the highest to the lowest, for every Chinaman, whatever else he may be, is a Confucianist at heart. We meet some great scholar who has just taken the highest literary degree in the empire, and who in time will be appointed a Viceroy of one of the provinces, and we ask him whom he considers to be the greatest teacher that the world ever saw. With a surprised look, he instantly answers: "Confucius, of course; who else could there possibly be?" He has studied his writings from his childhood. He knows every sentence and phrase in them by heart, and start him at any page in his works that you like,

A TEMPLE.

he will go on from chapter to chapter without the least hesitation or mistake till you choose to stop him. Confucius is the only inspiration that he has ever known. His thoughts have so permeated his life that to dream even of having any original ones of his own would be deemed an act of treason against the great sage worthy of the severest censure. We stop at a shop where the owner is sitting waiting for customers. We step in and ask him if he is a disciple of the great Confucius. He stammers out that the necessities of business have prevented him from studying his works with that care and attention that he would have liked; still he has not entirely neglected them, he says. He then rises, and from a shelf he brings down some volumes that look well thumbed, and sitting down opens one, and glancing through its pages chooses out some of his favourite passages. As he reads, his eyes begin to glisten, his voice naturally falls into a rhythmical chant, and his head sways from side to side as though impelled by the great thoughts that come to him from the page he is reading. He becomes absorbed; he forgets all about his business for the moment, and though crowds pass by his door, he heeds them not, for the spell of the words of the great master is upon him. We step out again into the street, and we come upon a coolie, hot and perspiring, standing by the great load he has just laid down, and we ask him what he thinks of Confucius. "He is the great sage and teacher of China," he replies, as he fans himself, whilst the perspiration rolls down his face. "I never had the happiness," he continues, "of being able to study his works like our scholars, but I have not entirely forgotten what I learned when I was a boy, and I can still repeat many sentences from his books. Confucius, you know," and here he becomes serious, and his fan is poised motionless in the air, "is the source of the learning and civilization of China. Without him our country would have been as barbarous as other nations, but to-day it is the most refined and cultivated in the world." The crowd, that has gathered round us, though composed of working men, vigorously applaud this statement. One voice after another is heard extolling his virtues, and declaring that the world has never yet seen his equal.

Confucius is the name that binds the empire into one. His writings have moulded the thought of the nation, and so enthralled its thinkers that no criticism of them is permitted, and no other standard allowed to be set up as of equal authority to them. Every scholar in the country is so by virtue of his having studied and mastered his works. He may have become proficient in every art and science in the world, but without a knowledge of them he will never obtain the coveted degree that is to open up the way to fame and wealth. As these scholars are the teachers of the youth throughout the eighteen provinces, and, moreover, occupy all the civil posts under government, it may be easily imagined how the current of thought and legislation is all Confucian.

The morality of the country is founded on the writings of Confucius. Even in religion there is no name so great as his. Buddhism after nineteen centuries of trial is dead in China, and has become lost in a mere system of idolatry. The Chinese don't look to it for morality, and if you were to ask the priest as he stands muttering before the wooden image, which he considers the greater, it or Confucius, he would, if he spoke what his heart felt, instantly reply, the latter. It has no doubt seemed marvellous that a people with such ability as the Chinese, and with such a wealth of natural resources should have remained stationary during so many ages, and that their gaze should have been so persistently towards the past. The fact is that time brings no growth to the nation. The nineteenth century, which is near its close with us, has not yet dawned upon it, but is still far off in the future. For ages the grip of the dead hand of Confucius has been upon the Chinese people, and long has the nation waited for one mightier than he who should unloose the fatal grasp and set it free.

With such a complicated and far-reaching system as this, one that touches the Emperor on his dragon throne, and to a greater or less degree every subject in his dominion, it would seem that Christianity would never be able to get a footing in China, for Confucianism and it could never exist side by side. Only one could reign. Now quite independent of our profound belief that the Gospel is to be the religion of the whole word, there are features about Confucianism that show conclusively that it has failed in a popular sense to be the religion of the people. It has no personal god, no future, no redeemer, and no answer to the thousand questions that the heart is always putting. Such a faith must in the long run inevitably fail. But even as a national religion that has grown with the growth of the nation, and whose roots are running throughout the whole of society, there is one aspect of it that shows its essential weakness. It has never yet touched the real *heart* of the people. Confucius has hitherto failed in exciting personal enthusiasm for himself. In all my intercourse with the scholars of China, I have not met with one that showed any passionate devotion for him. I don't believe there is a man in China that would go to the stake for him, or that would risk his life in any shape whatsoever for his sake, as thousands to-day would willingly do for Christ. His writings are cold and stately. They seem as though they were cut deep into granite slabs, and as we read, the chill from the stone drives out the warmth from our hearts. There is no loving heart beating behind them, no human sympathy, no tears, no poetry. They never make our blood run faster, or give us heroic thoughts; never fire us with an inspiration that makes us nobler and better men. One could never imagine an army, on whom the destinies of China hung, going into battle chanting some of his great sayings, and nerved by them to conquer or to die. In times of danger or of sorrow, or in the great crises of their national life, the last name the Chinese would dream of invoking is that of Confucius. The great void in the nation's heart has yet to be filled. Who can do that but Christ?

Forty-five years have passed away since the Mission was first established in Amoy. What experiences have been crowded into those years! Joy and sorrow sunshine and storm, have marked their course. Sometimes the heart has been gladdened with a success so great that sanguine hopes have filled it, that in a few short years the whole region would be Christianized. Then disappointment would come and dash these to the ground. Converts failed, and men that seemed as though they had been chosen of

God went back to heathenism, and stopped the work for years by their bad example. Then again the Gospel asserted its Divine power, and churches were formed, and men of heroic mould were elected of God to be apostles to their own countrymen. By and by the old heathen forces leagued together to stay the kingdom of Christ, and social pressure was brought to bear upon the Christians, and some unable to endure the strain bent before the storm, whilst the spiritual descendants of the men that in olden times went to the stake and the lions rather than deny Christ, stood firm, and thus proved themselves to be the true church of God. In all these years the Church has been steadily growing, until to-day it is a powerful factor in the moral and spiritual life of the people.

The Mission has now twenty-four churches, twenty-one of which invite their own preachers and pastors, and pay their salaries; one is supported by one of the native churches in Amoy, and the other is partially helped by the public funds at the disposal of the Mission. In connection with these twenty-four churches, there are twenty-two mission stations, ten of which are sustained by the natives, whilst twelve are aided partly by native funds and partly by money sent from England. In addition to the above, there are three preaching stations that were opened by the Mission, two in 1888, and one in 1885.

Besides the above, there are seven churches in the North River district. This work was commenced only in 1883, so that the success there has been very remarkable. Thus in all there are fifty-six churches and preaching stations where men assemble to worship God, and where the heathen can hear of the way of life.

The total membership of these is 1,478 adult members, 1,135 adherents, and about 400 baptized children, and during the year 1888 they subscribed for the maintenance of their preachers and pastors, and for incidental expenses the noble sum of 3,783 dollars. I may add that the English Presbyterian Mission, and the American Mission, have in connection with their churches a joint membership of 1701.

The story that has been told in the previous chapters, and the statistics with which I now close the book tell their own story. Which shall the nation choose, Christ or Confucius? Shall it be the great sage whose chilly hand has held the nation bound for all these ages, or shall it be the Son of Man, whose heart throbs with sympathy for every human being, and whose gentle touch, the inheritance of the Church, brings hope and comfort to men to-day? Need we doubt what the answer will be?

Butler & Tanner, The Selwood Printing Works, Frome, and London.

www.ingramcontent.com/pod-product-compliance
Lightning Source LLC
Chambersburg PA
CBHW020908230426
43666CB00008B/1357